American Legal Institutions
Recent Scholarship

Edited by Eric Rise

A Series from LFB Scholarly

The U. S. Court of Appeals and the Law of Confessions

Perspectives on the Hierarchy of Justice

Sara C. Benesh

LFB Scholarly Publishing LLC
New York 2002

Library of Congress Cataloging-in-Publication Data

Benesh, Sara Catherine.
The U.S. Court of Appeals and the law of confessions : perspectives on the hierarchy of justice / Sara C. Benesh.
p. cm. -- (American legal institutions)
Includes bibliographical references and index.
ISBN 1-931202-39-7 (alk. paper)
1. Confession (Law)--United States. 2. United States. Court of Appeals. 3. United States. Supreme Court. 4. Judicial process--United States. I. Title: United States Court of Appeals and the law of confessions. II. Title. III. Series.
KF9664 .B46 2002
347.73'24--dc21

2002008586

ISBN 1-931202-39-7

Printed on acid-free 250-year-life paper.

Manufactured in the United States of America.

To My Parents, Greg and Jayne Benesh, for everything

Table of Contents

Preface

Since beginning graduate school in 1995, I have been intrigued by the Courts of Appeals. First I was intrigued because of their institutional position. What does a federal court, charged with judicial review and policy making of all sorts, do when it's in a position in which it can be overruled, but hardly ever is overruled? Is there a real constraint there, and, if so, is it strong enough to actually influence their behavior? After some reading I was intrigued again to find that they actually do comply, nearly all the time. I simply had to figure out why! This book is an attempt at a preliminary answer to that question. With the odds stacked against it, it seems the U.S. Supreme Court gets compliance and has an impact, even though it's completely against the Courts of Appeals' interest at times and even though the Supreme Court does very little to induce that compliance. This puzzle is completely intriguing to me, and as I work through what I think may be a potential resolution, I hope it intrigues you too.

In this book, I discuss the confession cases in the U.S. Courts of Appeals, seeking to explain decision making in that area. In order to do so, I draw on principal-agent theory as it is related to the four major models of judicial decision making: the attitudinal model, the legal model, the strategic model, and the neo-institutional model. It seems to me that elements of all of these models are at work in the Courts of Appeals, none to the exclusion of the others. Attitudes matter as measured by political party affiliation of the panels; law matters as embodied by facts deriving from Supreme Court precedent; strategy matters as seen by the apparent desire to avoid reversal; and the institutional position of the lower court matters as it takes the Supreme Court into account in making its decisions. In short, these courts are complicated, as they deal with a myriad of influences the Supreme Court rarely thinks about. Their decision making is, sensibly, effected by these complications. So, we move from the extremely parsimonious attitudinal model explaining Supreme Court decisions, to this integrated and multifaceted one explaining Courts of Appeals decisions.

We have learned quite a bit about the Courts of Appeals in the last decade, but there is still so much more to figure out (see, e.g., *Law and Courts* 11(2):4-16). That is why this becomes such an exciting area of research. Research questions abound: How do these courts make decisions? Do they behave strategically? Are some circuits leaders and others followers? Which institutional aspects of the circuit courts cause the circuits to differ from one another? What are the trends over time in the agendas of these courts and how does that influence their behavior? Does it matter that some of them hardly ever publish their decisions? And how do they decide to hear a case en banc? This book touches only one aspect of the research agenda I see for these courts: sorting out their relationship with the Supreme Court. Obviously, there is much to be done in this area as well. All of this will be facilitated by the creation of the Court of Appeals Database (Songer 1998), the Attributes of Courts of Appeals Judges Database (Zuk, Barrow, and Gryski 1997) and the linkage between the two (Kuerston 2001). It is indeed an exciting time to be studying this topic and I hope current and future graduate students will take up the charge.

Acknowledgements

Since this is my first book, I don't know whether it's unusual or not to be indebted to a huge number of people in the research that has eventually culminated in this text. I assume it is not. Therefore, I'd like to take the time to thank some important people to me, both professionally and personally.

First, I thank my parents to whom this book is dedicated. They have always made me comfortable in the knowledge that I can do anything and they have always been my greatest supporters, every step of the way. I attribute my academic success (such that it is) to my mom for all the hours she spent reading to me as a child, and I attribute my work ethic (again, such that it is) to my dad, who works hard and is as meticulous (read, anal) a person as I have ever met. Additionally, I thank my dad for proofreading this manuscript. Having someone so meticulous (see above) is a real benefit when writing a book!

I also thank my brothers, Ben and Aaron, for being really great kids and for treating me so special all these years. It feels really good to know your little brothers look up to you and support you and are proud of you, especially when you feel the exact same way about them.

Even though I told him he wouldn't be getting thanked because he didn't help me code cases one late night in January, I guess I'll thank the love of my life too; albeit grudgingly. Seriously, Don is a great support to me and isn't afraid to tell me he's proud of me, or, as he puts it, that I'm a big deal. He is truly my anchor.

Academically speaking I have quite a few debts too, and the first one is by far the largest. Thank you Harold Spaeth, for being the best, most involved advisor on the planet (see Benesh 2001 for proof). I don't think I could have done any of this without him; in fact, I know I couldn't have. He was accessible to me no matter how much work he had and he has never once led me astray. His advice is always right on (when it comes to academics anyway!!) and he has always been brutally honest with me, which I hope reflects well in the work I've done that he has read and critiqued. He has also read this entire manuscript; once as a dissertation (well, more than once and more than one draft) and once now as a book. I know I benefit greatly from his substantive and stylistic comments and I only hope I do them justice in the final product. Most importantly, though, Harold has always treated me as a colleague; deferred to me when he thought I was right, sought my opinion on certain matters, and generally treated me as an equal. That meant so much to me as a graduate student, and means so much to me now. I'm very lucky to have had Harold as an advisor, and I feel extremely lucky to have him now as a colleague and, perhaps more importantly, as a friend.

Thanks to the wonderful, amazing, productive, collegial, and very much missed Department of Political Science at the University of New Orleans for support while starting this project, and to my new colleagues here at the University of Wisconsin – Milwaukee for support while finishing it.

Finally, thanks to my editor, Leo Balk, for his interest in my book, his belief that it was something worthwhile to pursue (despite my loudest cautions), and his patience with me and my aversion to deadlines. It's been a not too painful exercise.

Unfortunately, while I thank all of these people for help in some way on this project, I can't blame them for any mistakes in the manuscript. I really regret that.

Introduction

In attempting to explain the ways in which judicial actors decide, the literature on judicial decision making is pervaded with adherents of either the legal model or the attitudinal model (see, e.g., Segal and Spaeth 1993). Both tend to deny the operational relevance of the other, and a debate has ensued. Added to this debate are two other models of Supreme Court behavior: the strategic model (see, e.g., Epstein and Knight 1998 and Maltzman, Spriggs, and Wahlbeck 2001) and the neo-institutional model (see, e.g., Clayton and Gillman 1999). All of these models center around the U.S. Supreme Court and little work has been done to analyze decision-making tendencies of the Courts of Appeals to see if, in fact, the lower court judges decide cases compatibly with any of these models or a combination thereof. Indeed, we have only just begun to understand the empirical realities of these courts and their decisions (see, e.g., Songer, Sheehan, and Haire 2001). This book aims to increase understanding of decision making in the Courts of Appeals by examining the influence on it of the policy preferences of the judges, the legal context, the institutional environment, and the relationship between the Courts of Appeals and the Supreme Court.

I here assume that the lower court is constrained by its position within the judicial hierarchy, and that, as a result, a revised, integrated model of decision making applies to these courts. I test a modified principal-agent theory of judicial hierarchy which – I will show – nicely captures the interdependence of the two federal appellate courts. Due to the differential institutional make up of the two courts, we expect that decisions and decision-making processes will necessarily differ between them. Here, I test the presumption that, while the Supreme Court decides basically in a manner consistent with its policy preferences, the Court of Appeals must take into account other factors and other actors with which the Supreme Court need not concern itself. Its decision making is influenced by its relationship with the Supreme Court, its faithfulness to precedent, and its members' policy preferences.

This book employs several different methodologies to explore the components of decision making on the U.S. Courts of Appeals: (1) a simple formalization of the principal-agent relationship and utility maximization calculation for certain behaviors given certain preset probabilities; (2) probit models of decision making in the Courts of Appeals, including measures of the influence of Supreme Court precedent, Supreme Court ideological predisposition, and the policy preferences of the lower court judges; (3) a qualitative analysis of lower court response to two non-salient Supreme Court decisions in the area of confession (*Bruton v. United States* and *Townsend v. Sain*) to determine whether the lower courts actually comply or employ any number of creative non-compliance techniques; and (4) an individual-level analysis of the behavior of the three Supreme Court justices who also served substantial time on the Courts of Appeals, examining the same decision makers in different institutional environments to see if changing the rules changes the behavior of the players. Through these various exercises, I am able to at least partially examine attitudinal, strategic, legal, and institutional influences on Courts of Appeals decision making.

Using the foregoing methodologies and the theory of principals and agents, I show that decision making in the lower courts is influenced by the Supreme Court, but that the interaction between the two actors is quite different from principal-agent relationships that have been heretofore studied. The lower court heeds its principal not because of the direct supervisory function of the High Court – since that direct supervision is the exception rather than the rule – but rather out of a combination of legal factors, including role perceptions, legal norms, respect for precedent, and lack of clarity on the part of the Supreme Court. In other words, because of the hierarchical set-up of the judiciary, the lower courts *are* constrained by High Court pronouncement, but that constraint really has very little to do with what the Supreme Court *does* but rather what the Supreme Court *is*. While notions of "role" and "respect" are not readily operationalized, by demonstrating widespread compliance with Supreme Court decisions and the major impact that institution has on the decision making of the lower courts, coupled with the nearly total lack of Supreme Court supervision, I believe the inference can be validly drawn, if not scientifically demonstrated. In addition, I characterize the relationship as somewhat strategic in that attention to Supreme Court ideology demonstrates forward-thinking on the part of the Courts of Appeals in the guise of reversal avoidance. Finally, institutional differences are hinted at through an analysis of "judges turned justices." All of these demonstrate that the Court of Appeals jurist is differently constrained than the Supreme Court justice and, therefore, an integrated approach is necessary.

CHAPTER 1

The Hierarchy of Justice

1.1 Decision Making in the Supreme Court and the Courts of Appeals

Two models have dominated recent discourse on Supreme Court decision making. These are the legal and the attitudinal models. The legal model of decision making, as described by Segal and Spaeth (1993), adheres to the belief that "...the decisions of the Court are based on the facts of the case in light of the plain meaning of statutes and the Constitution, the intent of the framers, precedent, and a balancing of societal interests" (32). The attitudinal model, on the other hand, claims that "...the decisions of the Court are based on the facts of the case in light of the ideological attitudes and values of the justices" (32).

Because of the distinguishing characteristics of the Supreme Court one may conclude that the Courts of Appeals are different and therefore its judges may not rely solely on attitudes in their decision making. Segal and Spaeth address this possibility, and agree that a model of lower court decision making may necessarily differ, because lower court judges: 1) do not have the broad control of their docket the Supreme Court enjoys; 2) may desire higher office, thus exposing themselves to political influences; and 3) are subject to the superior Supreme Court, which has the authority to overturn their decisions.[1] In addition, these courts have a much heavier workload, and they may be more constrained by precedent, given their position in the judicial hierarchy. Strategic considerations may loom here as these judges attempt to avoid reversal. In short, legal, attitudinal, strategic, and institutional influences may be relevant. We must, therefore construct an integrated model; a goal to which this book aspires.

Why study the Court of Appeals? After all, most of the judicial literature to date explores any number of minutiae pertaining to the processes and decision-making tendencies of the Supreme Court, thereby contributing to the notion of Supreme Court primacy. Perhaps one should continue that research agenda, finding another aspect of Supreme Court decision making to more fully understand. While it is true that interesting questions remain at the High Court level, it is also the case that the lower federal courts (as well as the state courts, both appellate and trial) are increasingly becoming the focus of study. Most decisions are in fact decided within these courts. The Supreme Court's docket is shrinking while the number of appeals to it grow each year (Carp and Stidham 1996). This means that the Courts of Appeals (and state supreme courts) are almost always the last stop for justice; the Supreme Court formally decides less than 0.5% of the cases appealed to it (Songer, Sheehan, and Haire 2001:17). There is no question then, but that these courts are important institutions. It becomes imperative that we better understand how they make decisions. However, because of the institutional position of these courts, we still need to consider the influence of the Supreme Court on even those decisions in which it does not directly participate. The High Court is the supervisor of the lower courts. The lower courts are not completely free agents. Legal, institutional, and strategic considerations, along with attitudes, must be considered.

1.2 A "Principal-Agent" Theory of the Hierarchy of Justice

I propose a variation of the variation, if you will, of principal-agent theory advanced by Brehm and Gates (1997) in their book on bureaucracy and assert that the relationship between the Courts of Appeals and the United States Supreme Court can be well understood via such a theoretical construct. The High Court, by law, oversees the Courts of Appeals, and those lower courts are bound by the law as prescribed by that higher authority. This relationship, in turn, affects the means by which lower courts make decisions. While the assertion that the courts exist within a principal-agent relationship is not completely new (see, e.g., Songer, Segal, and Cameron 1994), I use it as a catalyst to derive and test expectations about Courts of Appeals behavior. Indeed, principal-agent theory naturally introduces aspects of all four models of judicial behavior when applied to this context.

Before delving into the theory of principals and agents, we should note that the judicial hierarchy does inherently differ from other hierarchies, and therefore, we should expect the judicial brand of principal agency to reflect this. Because of the character of this judicial hierarchy, some scholars are quite reluctant to grant worth to projects that employ this theoretical construct. However, that the theory does not fit exactly does not devalue its application completely. In fact, models are by design abstractions of reality; we do not expect reality to be totally represented within the model. Instead, we focus upon certain crucial factors, and glean as much from the model as possible. So, while the following sections describe principal-agent theory *qua* principal-agent theory, those sections which proceed from them explain the adaptations necessary to meaningfully apply such a theory to the relationship between the Supreme Court and the Courts of Appeals and, by extension, to the decision-making processes of the Court of Appeals judge, as well as describe the contribution such a model makes to the literature on lower court jurisprudence and our understanding of said decision making.

1.3 Principal-Agent Theory

An agency relationship, according to Eggertsson, "…is established when a principal delegates some rights…to an agent who is bound by a (formal or informal) contract to represent the principal's interests in return for payment of some kind" (1990:40). Miller and Moe define the principal-agent model as "…an analytical expression of the agency relationship, in which one party, the principal, enters into a contractual agreement with another, the agent, in the expectation that the agent will subsequently choose actions that produce outcomes desired by the principal" (1986:175). This relationship exists, then, within an hierarchical structure, which itself is a social choice aimed at correcting a market failure. Miller and Moe argue that any such relationship will result in a "Sen paradox" (180). Sen's paradox asserts that any organization which is decentralized (i.e. hierarchical) is subject to violations of Pareto optimality or transitivity, or, in attempts to maintain those attributes, must resort to constraining individual preferences.[2] In a hierarchical structure, actors may be both a principal and an agent simultaneously, creating an interesting dynamic.

The problem with the loyalty expectation of the principal – that is, the expectation of the principal that its will be done by his agents – is that it runs counter to the fundamental economic notions of self-interest (Songer, Segal, and Cameron 1994). Therefore, problems of enforcement arise. The agent, like the principal, has interests and the desire to act in accordance with those interests, unless subjected to substantial controls or inducements (Shepsle and Bonchek 1997). The difficulty, then, is the creation of enforcement mechanisms or incentive structures that will effectively constrain the actions of the agent in order to sustain an efficient equilibrium. Because those mechanisms will never be perfect, the possibility of shirking always exists.

Because of information asymmetry between the two, with the agent generally assumed to have more information than its principal, opportunity for the agent to "shirk" often occurs (Eggertsson 1990). Because of the costs of monitoring, the principal must make decisions as to which aspects it will supervise, and in what ways the outputs will be measured. A point is reached at which the principal will no longer gain utility from monitoring the agent, as the costs of monitoring will outweigh the benefits of compliance or some semblance thereof.[3]

These high costs of monitoring give rise to the possibility of moral hazards and adverse selection. A moral hazard, according to the principal-agent literature, arises when the principal measures compliance by some single proxy or indicator, thereby lessening effort in monitoring. This measurement method may allow for shirking in all other areas save the one which the agent knows will be monitored by the principal (Eggertsson 1990). Adverse selection, on the other hand, arises in the hiring of agents as principals attempt to rely on one easily identifiable criterion for hiring to save monitoring costs. For example, the principal may look only for applicants with a high college grade point average. In so doing, she may be missing other, better correlates of productivity, such as involvement in extra-curriculars or dedication to a certain cause as evidenced by volunteering. This adverse selection procedure may exacerbate the principal-agent problem by starting out with agents who may be more likely to shirk than like-qualified people.[4]

1.4 A New Model of Agency

Brehm and Gates, in their 1997 book on the bureaucracy, offer a useful permutation of the principal-agent model. They contend that prior theories of principal-agent relationships, or agency theories, are flawed in their assumption that agents will fundamentally shirk simply because they prefer shirking to working. They explicitly contend that agents will shirk only when they do not agree with the policy preferences of the principal. While this hardly seems a bold assertion, the literature in this area, especially that on the bureaucracy, never explicitly makes this point, preferring instead to paint the bureaucracy negatively. They assume that bureaucrats would much rather sit around and waste time than to actually get things done. Brehm and Gates provide evidence that this simply is not true.

Focusing on the problem of adverse selection, Brehm and Gates posit that, for some bureaucrats, compliance is the norm. The problem, then, comes in finding enough of these individuals. If that is accomplished, then the agency problem loses its bite. In describing those agents who do comply with their principal, Brehm and Gates assert that they do so because they share the preferences of that principal. Because previous work focuses on working and shirking, they fail to account for the "...positive efforts of policy-oriented bureaucrats, social workers with guiding agendas, police officers who honestly prefer to enforce the law, and professors who like to teach" (Brehm and Gates 1997:19). In order to make their point, they first identify the possible policy output decisions available to the bureaucrat: working, shirking, or sabotage.

"Some bureaucrats devote extraordinary effort toward accomplishing policy ("work"), where others may expend as much effort deliberately undermining the policy objectives of their superiors ("sabotage"). Other bureaucrats may be directing efforts toward non-policy goals ("shirking")" (Brehm and Gates 1997:21). In all three policy outputs, the main concern is what the policy goals are, and whether bureaucrats' actions are consistent with the preferences of the public, which should be approximated by the policy preferences of their principal.

Whether or not agents follow their principal, however, is not the only consideration Brehm and Gates consider. Another important question involves exactly who does the controlling. Bureaucrats, according to Brehm and Gates, are expected to enact the policy preferences of four different entities. The first is, of course, their supervisors or managers. The second policy preference which matters is their own. Bureaucrats obviously are influenced by their own policy preferences, and so this influence must be included. Bureaucrats also respond to one another, which is the third entity. Finally, bureaucrats respond directly to the public, the customers they actually serve (21).

Supervision, then, becomes very important in any discussion of agency. Brehm and Gates address the problems in the earlier literature as they attempt to add to the assumptions of the principal-agent model the possibility that shirking can take a number of forms; that supervision is costly; and that agents' preferences differ across issues, thereby making the propensity to comply differ across issues. "This model," they say, "is an enhanced principal-agent game emphasizing the choice of actions available to agents as they produce output and the constraints limiting a supervisor's authority over bureaucrats (the agents)" (1997:27).

Brehm and Gates spend some time on the supervisory problem, highlighting the fact that the enhanced principal-agent model supervisor is oftentimes unable to control his or her agent because of the many constraints s/he must face. There is the limited information constraint, the limited resources constraint, rules that constrain the supervisor, and the additional fact that the supervisor too has preferences and will allocate more resources to favored policy outputs. Therefore, both monitoring and sanctioning become very difficult. However, in this enhanced model, the preferences of the principal and the agent are the single best predictor of agency compliance. That being the case, supervisory problems may not be such an ominous concern, provided agents share the principal's policy preferences.

Besides the supervisor, as mentioned earlier, other actors may constrain the behavior of the bureaucrat, or at least influence it. One set of such actors is other bureaucrats, borne out in the creation of standard operating procedures. Brehm and Gates propound that, in order to better understand compliance, we must understand not only enforcement mechanisms and inducements, but also the history of the agency and the culture thereof, wherein "...workers learn from one another about appropriate behavior" (1997:48). They speak about more "peripheral" routes to compliance. That is, instead of a focus on the supervisory role of the principal, they focus on other influences on the agent which may also, in fact, induce compliance.

Under conditions of uncertainty it seems plausible to assert, as Brehm and Gates do, that people will look to others who are more expert than they in order to determine how they should act in a certain situation or react to a given stimulus. Applying that seemingly commonsensical notion, they extend the principal-agent model, for the first time it seems, to include other influences on agency compliance. These agents have networks and interact regularly with one another. That interaction is bound to have some influence on their behavior, and so must be included in our models of principal agency.

In addition to their influence on each other, Brehm and Gates also identify history as a constraint on agent behavior. This peripheral route to compliance asserts that an actor will look to his or her past behavior as a determinant of how to react to the current situation. Therefore, the first behavior of the individual and whether or not that behavior complied with the preferences and directives of the principal is most important. The problem becomes exacerbated, however, when changes in personnel occur; where a liberal principal with a given set of policy goals replaces a conservative principal with completely different sets of policy goals. In this situation, an agent complying with the first principal may be out of compliance with the second though performing identical tasks.

Summarizing, then, this brand of principal agency is primarily concerned with three ideas. First, agents will comply when their policy preferences coincide with their principal's policy preferences. Second, agents have an influence on one another and norms of behavior develop therefrom which are powerful constraints. The influence of history exacerbates this effect. Finally, monitoring matters, but it is not the end of the story if concurrent preferences and standard operating procedures (norms) work as they should.

This particular model of agency is particularly suited to a study of the courts. First of all, the concept that the agent will work, shirk, or sabotage according to his or her policy preferences and the degree to which those preferences coincide with those of the principal is essential in such a study. Since judicial decision making is generally agreed to be motivated by the policy preferences of the judicial actors, it is reasonable that the lower court judges would be more likely to follow their Supreme Court principal when their preferences coincide with the Court's decisions. Second, the notion that there are peripheral influences on the decision over whether or not to follow the principal is very useful to understanding the behavior of the lower courts. History, for example, in the form of adherence to precedent, or *stare decisis*, is at least given lip service by all lower court judges, so it should be included in a model which aims to determine the level of compliance by lower court judges to the policy prescriptions of the Supreme Court. Finally, the notion of inter-agent influence is one that we could apply to the judiciary as well. It seems plausible that the judges of the Courts of Appeals look to one another for guidance on how to behave, possibly measuring by their actions how to react to the Supreme Court, and thereby whether or not they should heed their principal. This could result in compliance norms and role perceptions which could effect behavior.

In addition, the enhanced problem of supervision also nicely explains the Supreme Court's position. The Court has resources limiting it to hear only a tiny fraction of all appeals coming to it. The High Court also has somewhat limited information on the performance of its subordinates, as it cannot plausibly know about every decision in every court. It knows only those appealed to it, and of those, it can only choose to hear a few. Finally, the influence of Supreme Court preferences comes to bear in its functioning as principal. Surely the justices care about certain policy areas more than they do others and, therefore, tend to hear those cases, making certain that the agents heed their policy prescriptions. This leaves a great number of potentially important issue areas under addressed by the Court. Its success as principal, then, depends quite heavily on devices other than direct supervision; devices like standard operating procedures and the influence of history.

The next section explores the fit of principal-agent theory to the judicial system in greater detail, highlighting instances where the theory proves to be quite helpful in understanding the relationship between the Supreme Court and the Courts of Appeals, as well as the influence that relationship has on decision making in the inferior court. I demonstrate the link between principal-agent theory and the four models of judicial decision making introduced above.

1.5 The American Judicial System as an Hierarchy of Justice

Studying the relationship between the Supreme Court and the Courts of Appeals as a hierarchical one seems both useful and plausible. Through use of this model, we can account for attitudinal influences both on supervision and on compliance, strategic considerations in attempts to predict and avoid reversal (which may also be considered institutional constraints), and legal influences established by the impact both of history (precedent) and inter-agent influence (norm construction).

How well does this construct really fit? In other words, is the relationship really one of a principal and its agents, or is it so different that it needs to be understood in some other way? In order to examine the question of appropriateness of the model to the judiciary, some important aspects of the model discussed both by Shepsle and Bonchek (1997) and by Miller and Moe (1987) will be examined, which demonstrate the unique relationship of the judicial hierarchy to this model.

In discussing bureaucratic drift, Shepsle and Bonchek list some possible control mechanisms that may be employed to deal with non-compliance, which calls to mind differences in the relationship between the Supreme Court and the lower courts on the one hand, and the bureaucracy-legislature on the other. In attempts to control actions of the Courts of Appeals, some mechanisms appear that are simply not available to the Supreme Court.

First of all, the appointment process is mentioned as a means by which a principal may control its agent, for it can thereby appoint or confirm those with similar policy positions. This possibility is not available to the Supreme Court, as the President nominates (and the Senate confirms) both the Supreme Court justices themselves, and their lower court counterparts. Therefore, the Supreme Court does not deal with the adverse selection problem that Miller and Moe point out as problems of monitoring, but does deal with the even larger problem of trying to control agents the Court was never given the opportunity to hire (or fire).[5]

Secondly, Shepsle and Bonchek discuss the creation of procedural controls, and again the Supreme Court is at a disadvantage in attempts to constrain the behavior of its lower court agents. In this case, it is the legislature which makes procedural changes in the administration of the judiciary when it sees fit, not the Supreme Court. Even if it wanted to, the Court could not itself change the rules of the game.[6]

In those instances in which the Supreme Court does exercise its monitoring duties and reviews decisions of the lower court, one can again see that the Court is constrained *by its very nature* from the enforcement capability of some other institutions. Shepsle and Bonchek (1997) describe the different oversight strategies of "police-patrol" and "fire-alarm" surveillance, mentioned earlier (see footnote 4). The Supreme Court is institutionally constrained to perform only the "fire-alarm" type surveillance, as it has neither the time nor the ability to patrol the lower courts to make certain that decisions are congruent with the decisional mandates of the Supreme Court. Instead, it must wait until a lower court makes a decision that the losing litigant deems to be worth the cost of appealing to the Supreme Court (which is rare), and which the Court moreover, deems important enough to review (which is rarer still). On the other hand, given the large number of cases appealed to the Court, one could assume that police patrol surveillance occurs as the Court wades through petitions arguably representative of all disputes and hears and decides those of most significance.[7]

The Court restricts the individual preferences of the lower court judges by overturning their decisions and resolving conflicts among the different circuits, but enforcement mechanisms are not systematic. This limitation provides more opportunity for shirking. Lower court judges no longer merely ask themselves whether or not they should decide cases a certain way, but rather whether they should decide them the way they want, even when that preference runs counter to the policy stance of the Supreme Court, and thereby risk possible reversal. More often than not that probability of review (let alone reversal) is close to zero.[8] On paper, it is easy to provide reasons for lower court avoidance of Supreme Court policy prescription. However, in reality, they almost always follow High Court pronouncements.

In a study designed to test such a principal-agent relationship between the Supreme Court and the Court of Appeals, Songer, Segal and Cameron (1994) use search and seizure cases, control for facts, and perform statistical tests to determine the extent to which lower court judges decide according to their attitudes, and the extent to which they regularly follow precedent set for them by their principal. They find that, while the Courts of Appeals are highly responsive[9] to the changing search and seizure policies of the Supreme Court, the judges also find opportunities to shirk in order to satisfy their own policy interests. They include variables measuring ideological changes on the Court, preferences of the lower court judge (utilizing an inferential measure with which there seemingly are a few problems, but none large enough to negate the importance of this variable), and the facts of the cases themselves.

Their model performs very well, predicting almost 90% of all cases, reducing error by 22%. They find a high degree of congruence with Supreme Court doctrine in the lower court. This congruence is not perfect, but is much closer to being so at both extremes (high probability of exclusion of evidence obtained in the search v. high probability of admission of evidence obtained in the search).

Secondly, they find that changing Supreme Court policy does have a substantial effect on the decisions of the lower court. Therefore, responsiveness is also seemingly present, even though lower court judges also follow their own policy preferences, thereby indicating an effect of Supreme Court policy and ideology, as well as the lower court judges' own ideology. They also find evidence for their contention that those cases not reviewed by the Supreme Court are those most likely to have followed the ideology of the High Court, thereby evidencing the influence of Supreme Court monitoring. The authors pithily summarize:

> As in the metaphor of the dog on the leash, some appeals court panels led and some followed "the owner," but when the Supreme Court tugged on the leash, both liberal and conservative panels were responsive (688).

There seems to be, then, some evidence of such a relationship. In order to further analyze both this relationship and decision making on the Courts of Appeals more generally, I extend their analysis using several different methodologies, a different set of cases, and a slightly different theoretical construct. Focusing on the relationship between principal-agent theory and the theories espoused by judicial scholars to explain decision making on the Supreme Court, I offer an integrated model of Courts of Appeals decision making, contending that it is necessarily more complicated and more inclusive.

1.6 Impact and Compliance Work

Additional evidence of the applicability of principal agency to the Supreme Court – Courts of Appeals relationship includes much of the impact and compliance literature. A prerequisite to the sort of analysis done by Songer et al. (1994) and that attempted here is that the Supreme Court have some influence on the lower courts. Many people have found substantial impact and compliance with Supreme Court decisions.

Indeed, it can no longer be said that the High Court's decision is the final decision (Wasby 1972). Lower courts exert some semblance of power over the Supreme Court in their interpretation and implementation of its decisions. However, mechanisms are arguably in place to undermine substantial deviations from the Court's prescribed policy, at least theoretically. Largely, though, it may be that lower courts will interpret cases consistently with Supreme Court intent only when they agree with that policy (or are indifferent to it), as Canon and Johnson (1999) contend.[10] Therefore, the principal-agent model of

Brehm and Gates may more aptly apply to the courts' hierarchical structure: the lower court will shirk when it doesn't like the policy, work when it does, and sabotage the policy when it really hates it (Brehm and Gates 1997).[11]

Canon and Johnson offer reasons for compliance by the lower court, akin to what Brehm and Gates find for the bureaucracy. First, the possibility of reversal deters the lower courts from shirking. While not many such reversals actually occur due to the Court's shrinking docket,[12] Baum finds that stigma attaches to one's reversal rate (1978; see also Baum 1976; Caminker 1994). Therefore, our concern about a seeming lack of monitoring by the principal may be overridden by the perspective the Court of Appeals jurist takes regarding her job performance. In addition, judges are socialized into the legal culture, thereby having certain role perceptions (Tarr 1977), and take a pledge to defend and uphold the Constitution, which should count for something (Canon and Johnson 1999). They also have an interest in maintaining the appearance of integrity in order that their decisions be accorded adequate respect, which would not occur if they blatantly disregarded Supreme Court policy. Or, judges could be acting solely out of self-interest, for in citing another's reasoning one does not have to reason oneself (Caminker 1994).[13]

However, a lower court needn't completely thwart Supreme Court precedent in order to influence its impact. In fact, the lower courts have several options available to them. They can interpret the decision narrowly, basically limiting it to its specific facts (Canon and Johnson 1999). They may cite their own opinions in lieu of citing the offending precedent (Manwaring 1972). They may attempt to distinguish their case from the one for which Supreme Court prescription is available (Caminker 1994; Songer and Sheehan 1990; Baum 1978; Tarr 1977; Manwaring 1972). They may dispose of the case on procedural grounds (Canon and Johnson 1999); they may criticize the Supreme Court while following it (Tarr 1977); or they may simply ignore the offending precedent's existence. (See Reddick and Benesh 2000 for a discussion of such behavior.)

One might expect that trial courts will be more successful in ignoring or defying precedent than will appellate courts, as the trial court judge's professional scrutiny is not as great as, for example, that of the Court of Appeals judge (Pacelle and Baum 1992). However, little evidence of outright defiance has ever been found in the intermediate federal appellate courts and most studies find widespread compliance (see, e.g., Benesh and Reddick 2002; Songer, Segal, and Cameron 1994; Songer and Sheehan 1990; Songer 1987; Gruhl 1980).[14] Many scholars posit that the Court of Appeals will be the most likely to comply with Supreme Court decisions, both due to its proximity to the Supreme Court, and its level of professionalism (Canon and Johnson 1999; Songer and Sheehan 1990; Gruhl 1980; Canon 1973; Murphy 1959). Of course, we still look to explain noncompliance, perhaps for the reason cited in Gruhl. "Just as there are relatively few stories about dogs biting people…but people who bite dogs are newsworthy, so it is that noncompliance with court rulings gets more attention than compliance, even though the latter may be more frequent" (1980:504).

1.7 The Necessity of an Integrated Model

So it seems, for whatever reason, the Courts of Appeals comply with the Supreme Court. We have the hook on which to hang principal-agent theory then. Given some semblance of Supreme Court influence, we should explain Courts of Appeals decision making with due regard to all relevant influences, legal, attitudinal, strategic, and institutional.

Attitudinal theory may travel to the Court of Appeals, although the use of attitudes will be tempered by the peculiar institutional constraints faced by the Courts of Appeals. These constraints include a heavy, albeit somewhat difficult to understand, strategic and institutional influence of the Supreme Court. Unlike the Supreme Court, more than just preferred policy needs to be considered. There is, therefore, no simple and parsimonious model of decision making in these more complicated courts (at least not as simple and parsimonious as the model that explains and predicts Supreme Court decision making). The Court of Appeals jurist takes several things into account, and to model her decision, we must look to a more complex formulation. Several scholars have quite convincingly argued for such an integrated model of judicial behavior (Songer and Haire 1992, Hall and Brace 1992, George and Epstein 1992). Therefore, I offer such.

My variation of principal agency includes all the necessary components of an integrated model of decision making. First, it incorporates the role of law, allowing for the influence of both vertical and horizontal precedent (history), role perceptions, and legal norms (inter-agent influences which manifest themselves in a seemingly irrational tendency to adhere to Supreme Court precedent). While doing so, however, this principal-agency offshoot does not forget the importance of attitudinal theory, incorporating into its formulation the ideological preferences of the judges on each court, and in so doing implies the institutional and strategic calculations made by Courts of Appeals judges regarding the probability of reversal. Therefore, this model offers a comprehensive representation of the process followed by lower court judges. The following chapters test this model using a variety of methodologies.

CHAPTER 2

A Model of the Relationship Between the Courts of Appeals and the Supreme Court

Chapter 1 suggests that the Supreme Court has an influence, but that influence may not be, by any means, direct. Formal theory offers us an attractive way to consider any relationship we desire to better understand, and it forces the researcher to consider scrupulously the assumptions he or she is making in studying a given relationship. Therefore, I employ a simplistic brand of formal theory to examine this principal agency to see if, by formalizing the relationship between the Court of Appeals and the Supreme Court, we can glean some explanatory power of which we can make good use in the methodological chapters that follow. I proceed in this chapter to examine the expected utility for the Courts of Appeals of shirking in preference to working (not following in preference to following), as well as the expected utility to the Supreme Court in supervising them, so that I may begin to put these principal-agency puzzle pieces together. In so doing, I formulate a judicial principal-agent game, complete with payoffs, to determine whether and when the lower court should, in theory, comply with Supreme Court policy pronouncements, or whether, in fact, it shouldn't.

2.1 A Simple Formalization of Judicial Principal Agency

Calculating expected utilities sheds some light on the choices that actors in a game are most likely to make. Here, I present inequalities[15] that must hold within expected utilities[16] for a given action to be taken by the lower court, and then by the Supreme Court. Through this exercise, we are able to exposit more clearly exactly those factors that should influence the decision by the lower court to comply, and by the Supreme Court to sanction or review. I use Brehm and Gates' principal-agent game, with a couple of modifications necessitated by my subject.

First, I do not posit a role for leisure shirking by the lower court (although such leisure is included in the payoffs calculated later).[17] While I think it plausible that such a goal (e.g., leisure) exists among lower court judges, as is the case for many human beings, the operationalization of this concept is fuzzy. One could plausibly define leisure shirking behavior as the court's desire to rid itself of as many cases as possible, thereby decreasing its workload. However, the lower courts have an almost fully mandatory docket, so the only way in which a lower court panel could "get out" of hearing a given case is to find some procedural grounds on which to dismiss it. However, I argue that finding procedural grounds for dismissal expends more effort than simply following whatever Supreme Court precedent is on point; hence the lower court would be making more work rather than finding a way to get a much needed break.[18] In fact, I would argue that if we are to accurately measure leisure shirking, such shirking would be found in the very cases in which the lower court follows Supreme Court precedent. After all, if the higher court already gives the answer, the lower court opinion author need not expend much energy in the opinion draft or legal reasoning. Because of these complications in the leisure shirking area, I decline to include such a consideration, including those times where the lower court rids itself of a case it doesn't like on procedural grounds, as a form of dissent shirking.[19]

The second modification of the Brehm and Gates formulation is that, for the lower court, dissent shirking and sabotage only differ in degree. Both avoid Supreme Court precedent. However, I define dissent shirking as a 'sneakier' sort of behavior, in which the lower court somehow *creatively* avoids the Supreme Court's prescription. I refer to this as creative noncompliance (see Benesh and Reddick 2002). If the lower court wishes to avoid following Supreme Court precedent, it has several options open to it. First, it may distinguish the facts of its case from the applicable precedent. This is perhaps the most popular form of defiance, although situations certainly exist where a lower court properly distinguishes its case from the Supreme Court precedent. Second, the lower court may declare the offending language in the Supreme Court case to be mere dicta, in which case it is not law. Third, the Court of Appeals may limit the applicability of the Supreme Court precedent to certain types of cases only, being sure to show why its case is not one of those types. And finally, the lower court can dispose of the case on procedural grounds, avoiding the merits altogether. All of these can be dissent shirking as the lower court defies the Supreme Court, deciding the case as it sees fit. However, when the lower court really disagrees with the Supreme Court and wishes to tell it so, the lower court may openly defy the Supreme Court. This I label sabotage, as the lower court is making its own policy regardless of its principal's earlier words on the subject. No longer is the Supreme Court's prescription the law in that case. Rather, the lower court has thwarted Supreme Court authority and made law itself. This indeed sabotages Supreme Court efforts to control that particular area of law.

Let the probability of the Court of Appeals (CA) following the High Court decision be f_{iCA} (i denoting the individual circuit), the propensity for dissent shirking be d_{iCA}, and the probability of sabotage be s_{iCA}. Supreme Court (SC) impact, then, will be a function of these probabilities and the effort expended by the Court for lower court supervision:

$$X_i = F_{iCA}(f_{iCA}, d_{iCA}, s_{iCA}, S_{SC}, \alpha_i, \delta_i) \qquad [1]$$

where X_i is the implementation of a given Supreme Court decision, S_{SC} is the effort expended in supervising decision making in the lower courts, α_i, is the probability of the litigants bringing an appeal, and δ_i includes external factors involved in the implementation of the decision that cannot be controlled by the Supreme Court (e.g., trial court non-compliance, other governmental actors' inaction in the implementation of decisions, miscommunication of the decision to governmental agencies, etc.).[20]

2.2 Compliance by the Lower Court

The Court of Appeals will follow the decision when

$\partial X_i / \partial f_{iCA} > 0$ implying, then, that [2]

$\partial X_i / \partial d_{iCA} \leq 0$ or [2a]

$\partial X_i / \partial s_{iCA} \leq 0$ or both [2b]

or, when the marginal utility of following the decision is greater than zero; e.g., benefits outweigh the costs in following the decision. Stated differently, when the marginal utility of dissent shirking or of sabotage is less than or equal to zero, the lower court is better off (or just as well off) following the Supreme Court prescription than trying to avoid it in some way.

The Court of Appeals will sabotage when

$\partial X_i / \partial s_{iCA} > 0$ and $\partial Xi / \partial d_{iCA} < \partial Xi / \partial s_{iCA}$ [3]

implying that

$\partial X_i / \partial f_{iCA} < 0$ [3a]

or, when the marginal utility of following the decision is less than zero and the marginal utility of sabotaging is greater than dissent shirking; e.g., it is less costly for the agent to work against the policy than it is for the agent to work for it or to dissent from it.

Finally, the Court of Appeals will dissent when

$\partial X_i / \partial d_{iCA} > 0$ and $\partial X_i / \partial f_{iCA} < 0$ [4]

but

$$\partial Xi / \partial d_{iCA} > \partial Xi / \partial s_{iCA} \qquad [4a]$$

that is, the agent gains more by shirking (creatively avoiding) than he gains by following the decision or by sabotaging.

The utility function for the Court of Appeals will then be

$$U_{CA} = F[X_i, (-P_{iCA})] \qquad [5]$$

(recall X_i's function in (1)) where X_i is compliance with the Supreme Court decision, and P_{iCA} is the punishment associated with noncompliance; namely, reversal by the Supreme Court. That punishment, then, is a function of the following:

$$P_{iCA} = F(S_{SC}, \alpha, \beta, \gamma, \varepsilon) \qquad [6]$$

where α, again, is the probability of appeal, β the probability of Supreme Court hearing (probability of granting certiorari), and γ is the probability of High Court affirmance.

The lower courts are assumed to have negative utility for compliance with disliked policies and for noncompliance (sabotage or dissent) with liked policies, and positive utility for compliance with liked policies or noncompliance (sabotage or dissent) with disliked policies, taking the risk of punishment into account.

2.3 Supreme Court Supervision

As [6] shows, the Supreme Court will not automatically supervise the lower court, but will attempt to maximize its utility, reviewing only the minimum number of lower court decisions in order to exact compliance from the lower courts. First though, we must consider the effect of SC supervision on lower court compliance.

$$\partial f_{iCA} / \partial S_{SC} = \eta(f_{iCA} - f^{*}_{iCA}) \qquad [7]$$

where f^*_{iCA} is the propensity to comply that the SC would prefer (which may be assumed to be 1), and η is a constant describing how susceptible each CA is to SC supervision.

Using this proposed effect of supervision, we can define the SC calculation of the worth of supervision as follows:

$$f_{iCA}|S_{SC} = f_{iCA}(\text{alone}) - (f^*_{iCA} - f_{iCA}(\text{alone}))(1-e^{-\eta S_{SC}}) \quad [8]$$

which simplifies to

$$f_{iCA}|S_{SC} = f^*_{iCA} - (f^*_{iCA} - f_{iCA}(\text{alone}))\, e^{-\eta S_{SC}} \quad [9]$$

and further

$$f_{iCA}|S_{SC} = 1 - (1 - f_{iCA}(\text{alone}))\, e^{-\eta S_{SC}} \quad [9a]$$

This amounts to the utility curve for SC supervision shown in Figure 2.1, which shows that, whether the CA under study is highly likely to follow given supervision or not, the effects of supervision diminish over time, assuming of course, that supervision leads to a higher likelihood of lower court compliance.

Of course, SC supervision may depend also upon the value it places on the particular decision currently up for compliance, and as the game progresses, implementation of the decision will be less desirable due to the discount factor.

2.4 Alternative Strategies at Work?

However, especially in the courts, we may find that direct supervision really plays a minute role. The Supreme Court tends not to hear cases. As stated earlier, it hears only 0.05% of all cases appealed to it each year (Songer, Sheehan, and Haire 2001). Therefore, there must be another factor not included here in the utility functions of the lower courts that can explain the broad compliance that has been found to exist. One such factor could be a legal role perception or socialization that would take the form of adherence to precedent and the perception of an inequality between the CA and the SC that should be resolved in favor of following SC pronouncements. This would mean that the preceding formulation of the model is incorrect; that instead of making utility maximizing choices, the CA instead relies upon a set of heuristics, as Brehm and Gates call them, in their decision making. These would be vertical and horizontal *stare decisis* (consistency), role perceptions (legal culture), and the observation of the behavior of other circuits (social proof). Where courts are concerned, I assume that the last two feed into a general "role" category and can be considered examples of inter-agent influence and the creation of standard operating procedures. The game tree that follows (see Figure 2.2) includes payoffs derived from such considerations, with the assumption that the Court of Appeals *wants* to avoid the Supreme Court decision. I assign cardinal numbers to the payoffs and solve for the "tipping point"; that is, the point at which the Court of Appeals will be indifferent between following a disliked precedent and not following it. Considerations included in the derivation of these rank-order payoffs include, for the Court of Appeals, policy preferences, adherence to precedent, conception of role, time spent in leisure, and the negative utility of being supervised. (Follow = More Leisure; Not Follow > Follow; Not Follow, No Appeal > Follow, No Appeal; Not Follow, Appeal, Not Review > Follow, Appeal, Not Review; Not Follow, Appeal, Review, Affirm > Follow, Appeal, Review, Affirm; Follow, Appeal, Review, Reverse > Not Follow, Appeal, Review, Reverse) .[21] For the Supreme Court, the payoff calculation includes policy preferences, power considerations, and leisure time, taking into account costs associated with supervision (Supervision = -Leisure; $\text{Power}_{\text{reverse}} > \text{Power}_{\text{affirm}}$; Policy > Leisure; Power > Leisure; $\text{Power}_{\text{review}} > \text{Power}_{\text{not review}}$). The outcomes are ranked from best (8) to worst (1). As I show, this decision depends on the lower courts' beliefs about the values of α, β, and γ; i.e., the lower court's beliefs that the parties to the suit will appeal, that the Supreme Court will take the case, and that the Supreme Court will affirm its renegade decision, determine the court's behavior.

The equilibria, then, depend upon lower court expectations of the likelihood of appeal, the likelihood of Supreme Court review, and the likelihood of reversal should the case be appealed and the Supreme Court see fit to hear it. The Supreme Court can manipulate those expectations by its behavior in order to exact lower court compliance should enforcement become necessary. More formally, we can set the expected utility of following equal to the expected utility of not following in order to find the point at which the lower court will switch from following to the more deviant not following behavior, as follows:

$$E(\text{Following}) = \alpha\beta\gamma(2) + \alpha\beta(1 - \gamma)(6) + \alpha(1 - \beta)(3) + (1 - \alpha)(4)$$

$$= -4\alpha\beta\gamma + 3\alpha\beta - \alpha + 4 \qquad [10]$$

$$E(\text{Not Following}) = \alpha\beta(1-\gamma)(1) + \alpha\beta\gamma(5) + (1-\alpha)(8) + \alpha(1- \beta)(7)$$

$$= 4\alpha\beta\gamma - \alpha - 6\alpha\beta + 8 \qquad [11]$$

Since these values are not easily interpretable, we might plug in values for α, β, and γ derived from the judicial politics literature.[22] We know that, at most, 20% of all cases are appealed to the Supreme Court (Carp and Stidham 1996). We can, therefore, assume that α=0.20. We also know that only one half of one percent of all cases appealed to the High Court are accepted for review there (Songer, Sheehan, and Haire 2001). Therefore, we set β=0.05. Finally, we know that the High Court is more apt to reverse the cases it accepts for review. In fact, it affirms only about one third of the cases it hears. γ, therefore, is set to 0.33 (Epstein et al 1997). Plugging these values into (10) and (11), we obtain the following expected values:

$$E(\text{Following}) = 3.8432$$

$$E(\text{Not Following}) = 7.7532$$

Again we find that these lower courts just should not be following Supreme Court pronouncements.[23] However, reality tells a different story and we therefore need to explain the difference between rational expectations and the legal reality. Possibly, the norm of vertical *stare decisis* overshadows the influence of many other considerations, including, perhaps, policy preferences. Or maybe the perception of role shared by judges tends them toward deference. The role perceptions I have included in the payoffs may not influence the judges to the same extent as, say, policy preferences; that is, perhaps role perceptions should be weighted more heavily. Somehow, the Supreme Court induces compliance, perhaps simply via valid authority. Or, on the other hand, perhaps policy preferences simply coincide between the Court of Appeals and the Supreme Court, and therefore elusive behavior is not necessary. Any of these factors seem to provide a plausible explanation for the incongruence between the theoretical expectation and reality. A completely different, yet plausible, solution to the puzzle is that studies finding conformity by lower courts overlook what I label 'creative non-compliance.' Such behavior oftentimes looks like compliance and may consistently be underestimated, producing the appearance of deferential behavior. If this be the situation, little difference exists between our theoretical expectation and reality.

In the remainder of the book, I attempt to sort out these difficulties. First, I determine whether or not the courts do have coincident preferences. Then, I determine whether Supreme Court precedent (legal influence) and ideology (strategic and institutional influence) effects Courts of Appeals decision making in one set of cases (confession cases from 1946 – 1981). Additionally, I test for creative noncompliance by tracking the treatment of a couple of non-salient Supreme Court cases. Finally, I look more closely at institutional influences on the Courts of Appeals by examining the behavior of judges on the Courts of Appeals later elevated to the Supreme Court. I draw some conclusions from my results and provide directions and thoughts for future research in the final chapter. All of these foci seek to determine if and when the lower court defers to its principal, and, in the end, why. If we confirm that the lower courts are indeed faithful agents, while recognizing that Supreme Court review is highly improbable, we necessarily establish a new variant of the principal-agent relationship: one in which the mere precedence of the principal, coupled with strong standard operating procedures, induces agency compliance.

Figure 2.1: Utility Curves of the Courts of Appeals

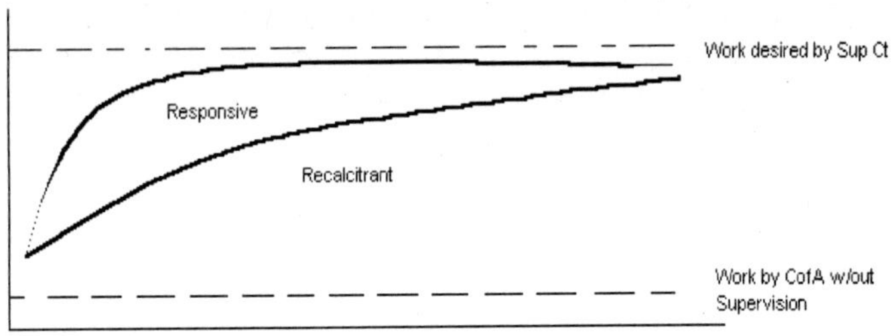

Figure 2.2: Game Tree – Principal Agency in Action

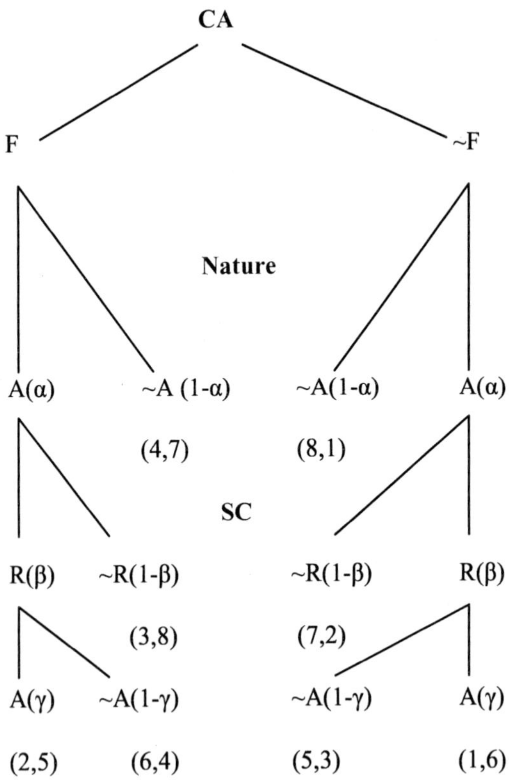

CHAPTER 3

Confession Cases in American Courts

In order to test the notion of judicial hierarchy and to model explicitly the decision making of the Court of Appeals, and because of a need to include measures of Supreme Court precedent and to standardize decisions across circuits, we need to focus on one particular issue area. I have chosen confession cases and in this chapter I present the arguments for their utility, the history of their treatment in the Supreme Court, and the development of the law of confession. I then turn to issues of case selection, validity, and reliability, as well as briefly discuss the methodological tool I use to measure Supreme Court precedent (fact-pattern analysis), finally delineating the facts to be coded here and the rules used in that coding.

3.1 Cases Involving Confession: Their History and An Argument for Their Use

I examine the confession cases for several reasons. First of all, pragmatically speaking, there are enough cases in both the Supreme Court and in the Courts of Appeals to undertake a sound and rigorous analysis.

Second, in this area of the law, differences in fact contribute mightily to the Court's decisions. The Supreme Court itself has indicated as much (see *Haynes v. Washington*[24]) and it is notable when reading these cases how carefully documented the relevant facts are.

Choosing a single area of the law in which differences in fact beget differences in outcome, at least theoretically, we obtain a good measure of lower court attention to precedent, as a given Supreme Court precedent in this area of law can generally be seen to add or subtract a given factor to or from the voluntariness consideration.[25]

To examine congruence, it is also necessary that the issue area under study include significant change in Supreme Court doctrine over time (Songer, Segal, and Cameron 1994:677). Confession fits that consideration as *Miranda* and *Escobedo,* among others, clearly changed the Court's doctrine and thereby brought many cases with potential for the application of new Supreme Court precedent to the dockets of the Courts of Appeals. Mapping the influence of those facts on Courts of Appeals decisions becomes an indicator of two things: the role of precedent (when interacted with Supreme Court decision dates), and the influence of the Supreme Court on the Courts of Appeals (where facts said to be important to the Supreme Court are similarly important to the Courts of Appeals).

Finally, other scholars have recognized the utility of fact pattern analysis in this area. Fred Kort, for example, identifies a long list of considerations to which a court responds when deciding whether a confession was so involuntary as to warrant reversal (1963:137). These include defendant characteristics as well as the tactics employed to obtain confessions, including physical and psychological coercion.

3.2 The History of Confession

Otis Stephens systematically examines how the Supreme Court has attempted to balance social order and individual rights in the area of involuntary confessions (1973). In his study, he delineates the history of the amendments related to confessions, the "fair trial" doctrine, the *McNabb-Mallory* rule, and finally, the impact of *Miranda* and the controversy surrounding that decision. I derive much of the following from his excellent treatment of the subject.

As we know, the protection against police coercion of confession is afforded to U. S. citizens through a combination of the Fifth Amendment's immunity against compulsory self-incrimination, the

Sixth Amendment's right to the assistance of counsel, and the Fourteenth Amendment, which made the aforementioned applicable to the states. The Supreme Court has used these amendments to justify its activism in the area of police interrogations and confessions. Of course, the Court has not always been so willing to associate these amendments with procedural protections of the accused.

Indeed, the earliest basis for Supreme Court policy making in confession cases is the English common-law rule excluding involuntary confessions, designed primarily to guard against the introduction of unreliable evidence. It was not aimed at objectionable interrogation practices, but at the protection of the accused from an unjust conviction (Stephens 1973). Using this rule, courts looked to the circumstances of the confession, along with the evidence surrounding guilt to determine if the admission was true. If it was true, no harm was done regardless of the treatment.

During this time, the U.S. Supreme Court reviewed only those convictions based on physically coerced confessions, directly condemning the police-inflicted "third degree."[26] This protection did not reach very far, for the Court also recognized the common law "evidentiary rule" which stressed the reliability of the confession. With this rule, "third degree" questioning may not affect admissibility if the accused did in fact commit the crime, as evidenced by other facts presented at trial.

In the 1920s the Court began to focus on a policy that was much more concerned with the fairness of the trial than with whether or not the accused actually committed the crime. In other words, the concern began to become due process, excluding from admissibility confessions that may have even been true, but nonetheless were improperly obtained. This has been dubbed the "fair trial" doctrine, which replaced trustworthiness in the determination of the admissibility of confessions. Justice Louis D. Brandeis quite nicely articulates this doctrine in a dissent:

> At the foundation of our civil liberty lies the principal which denies to government officials an exceptional position before the law, and which subjects them to the same rules of conduct

> that are commands to the citizen...Respect for law will not be advanced by resort, in its enforcement, to means which shock the common man's [sic] sense of decency and fair play.[27]

The so-called "judicial revolution" of 1937 increased the pace of Supreme Court activity in the field of confessions, as well as in other areas of criminal procedure, and in freedom of expression and race relations, reflecting its growing concern with the protection of individual rights (Stephens 1973). During this judicial revolution the Court struggled to attempt to define the "fair trial" doctrine. Defining the scope of constitutional limitations on police conduct is difficult, since the Constitution does not really speak to police conduct in obtaining confessions at all. Instead, the requirements of a fair trial relied for constitutional legitimacy on the concept of due process. The Court looked at such factors as public interest or excitement, the atmosphere surrounding the trial, characteristics of the defendant, and effectiveness of counsel to determine whether a given proceeding was fair or not (Stephens 1973), thereby considering both legal and extralegal factors.

The first major case in which the Court invoked the fair trial standard was a very easy one out of Mississippi.[28] In this case, three black men were severely whipped in order to obtain their admissions about a murder. The Court found that the extreme physical coercion preceding the confessions of these three rendered their confessions inadmissible and their convictions invalid. Justice Hughes wrote for a unanimous Court, indicating that the ruling rested on the requirements of due process, and not on the protection against self-incrimination. Applying the "fair trial" doctrine, Hughes argued that, because the wrong done to the defendants was so fundamental, it "made the whole proceeding a mere pretense of a trial" rendering the resulting conviction and sentencing completely void (at 286). This decision opened the door to review of police practices and the protection of prisoners, even if that opening was slight.

In the late 1930s, the Court began to extend the protections accorded to the accused, determining first whether or not coercion occurred, and later extending the scope of what constituted coercion. The Court no longer relied only on reports of physical violence, but exonerated the accused on the basis of psychological coercion as well, balancing the amount of pressure exerted by police against the capacity of the suspect to handle that influence. Justice Black eloquently sums this up in *Chambers v. Florida*:

> Under our constitutional system, courts stand against any winds that blow as havens of refuge for those who might otherwise suffer because they are helpless and weak, outnumbered, or because they are non-conforming victims of prejudice and public excitement. Due process of law, preserved for all by our Constitution, commands that no such practice as that disclosed by this record shall send any accused to his [sic] death. No higher duty, no more solemn responsibility rests upon this Court, than that of translating into living law and maintaining the constitutional shield deliberately planned and inscribed for the benefit of every human being subject to our Constitution -- of whatever race, creed, or persuasion.[29]

In 1943, the Court introduced a separate standard of confession for federal cases by focusing directly on police procedures, greatly widening the scope of judicial surveillance over the interrogation process. The McNabb-Mallory rule, named for the two cases that established it,[30] provided that an accused person be promptly arraigned before a judicial officer, with any testimony obtained beforehand excluded from trial. This broadened the due process requirements of confession admissibility well beyond the "fair trial" doctrine.[31] Justice Frankfurter summarized the rationale in *McNabb*:

> The history of liberty has largely been the history of observance of procedural safeguards. And the effective administration of criminal justice hardly requires disregard of fair procedures imposed by law.[32]

In *Mallory* the Court explicitly set forth the meaning of the "prompt arraignment" requirement, attempting a definition of "unnecessary delay."[33] The Court did not outlaw police questioning, but it did insist on at least a semblance of judicial surveillance of all detentions. Appearance before a magistrate ensured that suspects were informed of their right to remain silent and to the assistance of counsel. These decisions elicited great resistance from law enforcement and those within the government sympathetic to the police, as the federal standard in particular had, they argued, no real Constitutional basis.[34]

During the 1940s, the Court had difficulty endorsing one single position on confessions, oscillating between Black's earlier-mentioned test of "inherent coerciveness" (see note 28) and the traditional "fair trial" doctrine. When Justices Clark and Minton joined the Court in 1949, a new majority put an end to judicial activism in the area. These conservative justices created a majority who began to ease Fourteenth Amendment restrictions (Stephens 1973).

This conservative phase was short lived, however. The Warren Court, beginning in 1953, expanded constitutionally guaranteed protections of individual liberties. The Court began to consider the "totality of circumstances," deciding the admissibility of confessions on a case by case basis with the notion of impermissible coercion broadly defined.

Justice William O. Douglas urged the linkage of the right to counsel with the ban on coerced confessions during this time. He argued in *Crooker v California*[35]:

> The mischief and abuse of the third degree will continue as long as an accused can be denied the right to counsel at this the most critical period of his ordeal. For what takes place in the secret confines of the police station may be more critical than what takes place at the trial (at 444).

Douglas' view prevailed in the early 1960s with the formal repudiation of the "trustworthiness" principal. Convictions based on involuntary confessions, whether the confessions were true or not, could not stand, for, according to Justice Frankfurter: "...ours is an accusatorial and not an inquisitorial system..."[36] In 1964, due process was extended to include the Fifth Amendment's protection against self-incrimination.[37]

The application of additional provisions of the Bill of Rights to the states produced a revolution in criminal procedure. In 1961, the Court decided *Mapp v Ohio,* and in 1964, *Escobedo v. Illinois.*[38] The former protected against unreasonable searches and seizures, while the latter made inadmissible any confession obtained if an accused requested and was denied counsel.

Miranda v. Arizona[39] dispelled any uncertainty resulting from *Escobedo*. The Court, creating standards applicable to both state and federal prosecutions, spelled out the necessary warnings that were to precede an arrest, including: 1) the right to remain silent; 2) an explanation that anything said can and will be used against the accused; 3) the right to consult with an attorney who may be present during interrogation; 4) the explanation that, if the accused cannot afford an attorney, one will be appointed free of charge; and 5) if the suspect wishes to waive his or her right, s/he may nonetheless assert the right to remain silent or request counsel at any time during the course of the proceeding, at which time interrogation must cease. The Court further stated that "...a heavy burden rests on the government to demonstrate" that, if a defendant does waive his or her rights, s/he did so "knowingly and intelligently."[40] The Court concluded that the atmosphere and act of questioning is inherently coercive, agreeing with Justice Black's earlier opinion, and so worked harder to protect the accused from making uncounseled and unintended statements. The Warren Court was not completely consistent in its decision making in this area, however (see, e.g., *Boulden v. Holman*[41]), and, with the arrival of Chief Justice Burger, standards were further relaxed. For example, while Warren opposed any use of a coerced confession, Burger, writing for the Court in *Harris v. New York,*[42] stated that "It does not follow from *Miranda* that evidence inadmissible against an accused in the prosecution's case in chief is barred for all purposes, provided of course that the trustworthiness of the evidence satisfies legal standards."[43] He argued that an involuntary confession could constitutionally be used in court to impeach the testimony of the defendant should s/he choose to take the stand.

Overall, this area of law is surely characterized by the notion that the facts matter and by a piecemeal decision-making process in the Supreme Court, as it examined, case-by-case, which facts were to be considered in the voluntariness decision. This process created precedent to be followed in the lower courts, and hence provides an opportunity to test Supreme Court effectiveness. Israel and LaFave (1971), as well as Ringel (1966), identify some of the most important developments in the case law. *Haynes v. Washington,*[44] for example, established that voluntariness required the examination of the "totality of circumstances" surrounding a confession and prior case law determined what the relevant circumstances might be: 1) physical abuse;[45] 2) threats;[46] 3) extensive questioning;[47] 4) incommunicado detention;[48] 5) denial of the right to consult with counsel;[49] and 6) characteristics and status of the suspect.[50] Because the High Court has decided so many of these cases and because it often took cases specifically to rule on the influence of one given fact, it seems defensible to use the influence of these prescribed facts as measures of the influence of the Supreme Court and its precedents on the Courts of Appeals, which is what I do here.

This area of the law should prove instructive in enhancing our understanding of judicial decision making. The general public deems it important, as countless public opinion polls report exasperation when a reputedly guilty person goes free simply because "the constable blundered."[51] Finally, scholars deem it important, evident by the wealth of writing about the confession cases, especially *Miranda.*[52] The character of the facts that lead the Court to affirm or reverse a conviction on the basis of an improperly obtained confession provides a basis by which to test the larger theoretical questions presented here.

3.3 Defining the Universe

I use a "legalistic" approach to identify the universe of cases for this project. This defined universe was obtained by using West's Key Number system. Many cases involving a confession turn on considerations independent of the confession. The Court, moreover, uses widely varying language. It was therefore apparent that a LEXIS search would not be feasible. I also considered utilizing *Shepard's Citations* in conjunction with Spaeth's confession cases (Spaeth 2002), but was not happy with that prospect either, due in part to criticism of *Shepard's* as a selection tool (Songer 1988).[53] Therefore, I settled upon West's *Decennial Digests*, taking every case under keys 516 through 538 decided between 1946 and 1981[54] in both the Supreme Court and the Court of Appeals. These keys are under the larger subject of

"Criminal Law," under the heading "Evidence" and the subheading "Confessions." The title of each of these keys is listed in Table 3.1. Because West Publishing Company has a very good reputation, evidenced by the wide use of their products in the legal community, I view their listing to be exhaustive and validly and reliably constructed. These at least were a defensible universe of cases. I assume any omitted cases are randomly distributed and are not systematically related to admissibility, having no systematic fact pattern.

3.4 Fact-Pattern Analysis

Fact-pattern analysis has been utilized in different forms and in different issue areas for many years. Only recently has this method been theoretically infused (Songer, Segal and Cameron 1994). The method itself relies on the assumption that differences of fact beget different outcomes. It has been noted over time (although not empirically) that a very small difference in the facts of a case may substantially impact a decision. It is important to note, though, that I am not advancing a fact-based model of either courts' decision making. Rather, I attempt to test for the influence of the Supreme Court on the Court of Appeals by coding the presence or absence of relevant facts. In other words, do the facts that the Supreme Court has identified as being relevant considerations in the determination of voluntariness matter to the decisions of the Courts of Appeals? If so, we have an indication that the decision making of the Supreme Court matters to the Courts of Appeals. If not, it seems the lower court is paying little heed to its principal.

Many scholars have used this type of coding to predict court decisions. Kort (1957, 1958, and 1963) recognized the inherent benefit of studying appellate court cases by analyzing the different patterns of fact apparently guiding the judges' decisions. While his work perhaps lacked methodological rigor (Fisher 1958), it was theoretically useful, as it outlined a method to quantitatively predict court decisions. His work is additionally useful to this author as Kort (1963) used the confession cases and so set out a list of facts relevant to the Supreme Court's decision making in that area. His Table 1, which is reproduced here as Table 3.2, lists the facts which he deemed important to decisions in involuntary confession cases. I draw on his list for my model (see Table 3.3).

Segal (1984, 1986) also employed fact patterns and found that, in search and seizure, the facts of the cases did affect the decisions reached.[55] Hagle continued this line of inquiry with a fact-pattern analysis of the Court's obscenity cases (1991) and Ignagni studied free exercise cases in a fact-pattern model (1990).

Utilizing the confession cases, this project codes for the presence or absence of a defined set of facts handed down by the Supreme Court as important to the determination of voluntariness. There are admittedly theoretical difficulties in using facts to predict decisions. Indeed, some argue that the inclusion of controls for facts is atheoretical. Many argue that what a fact-based model really measures is the influence of Supreme Court precedent. However, I argue that, because I *am* using the fact-pattern methodology specifically as a measure of Supreme Court precedent, and my theory is not that facts affect Supreme Court decisions but that Supreme Court facts affect Courts of Appeals decisions, any criticism of the fact-pattern method applies little, if at all, to my project. This is a different type of fact-pattern model, and a different way in which to model court decisions, and I think its use is readily defensible.

The following section identifies the facts that were coded (again, as realizations of measurable Supreme Court influence) and discusses the validity and reliability of the coding.

3.5 The Facts

I carefully determined the facts to be coded by consulting many sources on the law of confession. There are many considerations on which the determination of the voluntariness of a given confession may turn. To settle upon the set of facts presented in Table 3.3, I consulted Kort's work, other sources on confessions and the admissibility thereof (e.g., Inbau and Reid 1962; Schafer 1968; Rutledge 1994), and the Supreme Court decisions themselves. In reading the cases contained in my analysis, I identified certain facts delineated by the Court as things to be considered when determining voluntariness. Those facts, which are listed in Table 3.3, are described here in more detail, with the specific coding scheme employed shown in Table 3.4.[56]

First of all, actual coercion is expected to be an important fact in the determination of voluntariness. Where coercion is present, manifested either physically (e.g., *Brown v. Mississippi, Lee v. Mississippi*) or psychologically (e.g., *Payne v. Arkansas*), the court will more likely overturn the confession.[57]

Forms of coercion other than those explicitly physical or psychological exist; those are also coded. Deprivation of basic needs includes lack of food or sleep for the defendant (e.g., *Davis v. North Carolina*). Again, we would expect their presence to increase the likelihood of excluding the confession. Length and place of detention are also coded as coercive forces, since a lengthy detention, or any detention in squalid conditions, also adds to the pressure brought to bear on a defendant (see again, *Davis v. North Carolina*). The longer the detention, especially in conjunction with a failure to bring the accused before a magistrate, (which will be discussed shortly), the more likely is the confession's exclusion. Similarly, the conditions of that detention may contribute to the likelihood of exclusion. If the defendant were held incommunicado; that is, without the assistance of family, friends, or an attorney, we would also expect the atmosphere to be additionally coercive, thereby enhancing exclusion (e.g., *Payne v. Arkansas*). Finally, the presence of an attorney has been determined to mitigate coercion. Therefore, if an attorney represents an accused, we expect the court to be more likely to uphold the confession (e.g., *Fay v. Noia*). If an accused requests an attorney and that attorney is denied, however, we would expect the court to be much less likely to uphold the confession, since an important right was not only ignored, but also actively thwarted (e.g., *Escobedo v. Illinois*).

In addition to these coercive forces, I have identified several characteristics of the accused which may lead that individual to be more or less affected by coercive methods (see, e.g., *Culombe v. Connecticut, Gallegos v. Colorado, Spano v. New York, Davis v. North Carolina, Harris v. South Carolina, Stein v. New York*). These include mental status, intelligence, race, experience, youth, and some other miscellaneous characteristics.[58] We would expect a defendant with a mental illness or defect to be more vulnerable to coercion than another like situated defendant. In addition, we would expect a defendant of subnormal intelligence to be more easily coerced than an intelligent defendant. We may expect that a defendant of a minority race to be more susceptible to subtle coercive tactics than a defendant of a majority race since the interrogator(s) may be more intimidating. We would similarly expect a young defendant to be more vulnerable. On the contrary, legally experienced defendants should be less susceptible to police coercion.

I have also identified some procedural defects that may taint the voluntariness of a confession. These include things that the police are supposed to do or have power over, that assure the fair treatment of an accused; e.g., the reading of the *Miranda* rights (e.g., *Miranda v. Arizona*) (or informing suspects of constitutional rights before *Miranda*); the length and place of interrogation (e.g., *Turner v. Pennsylvania*); the use of police relay tactics in questioning (e.g., *Haley v. Ohio*); and the bringing of the defendant before a magistrate without unnecessary delay (e.g., *McNabb v. U.S., Mallory v. U.S.*). Most of these are self-explanatory. A confession obtained via a long interrogation in a dingy room without windows by a large number of officers serially and in tandem is more likely to be overturned than is one in which the defendant is questioned over a very short time in a light and airy room by one investigator. Similarly, a defendant who is given his or her rights by a magistrate and formally charged with the crime he or she is accused of committing is more likely to avoid coercion than is a defendant who is badgered into confessing before seeing a judge. I also code for the voluntary waiver of *Miranda* rights (e.g., *Miranda v. Arizona*), as such a waiver would obviously mitigate a claim of coercion.

In addition to these facts, I have also coded mitigating circumstances, introduction of a codefendant's confession (e.g., *Bruton v. U.S.*), courtroom procedural fairness (e.g., *Jackson v. Denno*), habeas corpus petitions, the determination of harmless error (e.g., *Chapman v. California*), prior coerced confession (e.g., *Silverthorne Lumber Co. v. U.S.*), and fruits of illegality (e.g., *Wong Sun v. U.S.*). The mitigating circumstance variable could be somewhat gross, but I have defined it carefully. I coded this variable as being present when factors serving to mitigate the involuntariness of the confession were established in the record. These include such considerations as the differences between state law and federal requirements, those questioned while in custody on another unrelated charge, and those who personally increased the amount of time between arrest and presentation to a magistrate. This variable, when present, may help explain why a seemingly involuntary confession is upheld. Courtroom procedural fairness refers to the determination of voluntariness by the court. Early confession law submitted to the jury the question of the voluntariness of the confession. However, it was later established that the judge must make a separate determination of voluntariness outside the presence of the jury in order to avoid prejudicing the jury (*Jackson* v. *Denno*, 378 U.S. 368 (1964)). If such a hearing was held and the judge's findings are clear from the record, the procedure was fair; otherwise it may influence the admissibility of the statement.

The fruits of illegality variable is present when the court has either determined that the arrest and/or detention of the defendant was illegal or evidence was obtained during an illegal search, and the confession is a fruit of one of these illegal actions. If an earlier confession was deemed to have been obtained illegally, I code for the presence of prior coerced confession, expecting that such a subsequent confession will be deemed involuntary as a fruit of the first. Harmless error is coded as present only if the judge (or panel) decides that an infraction in criminal procedure did not lead directly to the conviction and so was excusable, or harmless. This factor should also serve to mitigate a finding of involuntariness. Finally, I include a variable for habeas corpus as a control to see if there is a difference in the way in which habeas petitions are handled (versus a regular appeal). Each of these factors plausibly contributes to the likelihood function for the decision of the court, either negatively or positively, depending on the expected relationship. (See the Table 3.4 for specific coding decisions.)

For each fact to be coded, I follow a trichotomous coding scheme, using the facts as stated by the appellate court that made the decision. I have coded each particular fact as "mentioned as present," "mentioned as not present," and "not mentioned." This addition to the Songer et al model should provide additional germane information; specifically, it will permit analysis of factors present in the given case as well as those which are mentioned by the court as *not* being present in the case at hand. Each should affect the likelihood that the confession will be overturned. One would think the former to be a bit more important, but it makes perfect sense that the mention of the absence of facts is also important or judges would not engage in such behavior. The model also contains a variable controlling for the ideology of the court under study (measured as the percentage of Democratic judges on the panel), as well as a control for the lower court disposition, since, unlike the Supreme Court, the Courts of Appeals tend to affirm the lower court decision under review.[59]

Reliability tests were conducted, and the results were quite satisfying. Of the 5% sample coded by the additional coder, 97.7% of all cells were identical to my coding. In 84.3% of the non-zero cells, we agreed (with most disagreements a matter of simple misunderstanding of the coding rules) and in 99.3% of the cells containing a zero there was agreement. This provides good evidence of the accuracy of my coding. As far as validity is concerned, the careful construction of the coding scheme along with the extensive use of legal scholars' identification of relevant case facts in confession cases (e.g., Criminal Justice Institute 1976; Grano 1996; Inbau and Reid 1962; Israel and LaFave 1971; Ringel 1966; Rutledge 1994; Schafer 1968; VanMeter 1973; Wigmore 1942) bodes well that I am neither missing any substantively important facts, nor am I including any irrelevant to the decision made in a confession case. In short, there is evidence that my data were validly and reliably coded. The next chapter analyzes these data in order to test our notions of the hierarchy of justice and the relevance of the attitudinal, legal, strategic, and institutional models to U.S. Courts of Appeals decision making.

Table 3.1: West's Key System - Criminal Law - Evidence[60]

K. Confessions.

Key 516. Nature and sufficiency as admissions of guilt.

517. Admissibility in general.
- (1). In general.
- (2). In particular criminal prosecutions.
- (3). Necessity of laying predicate for admission.
- (4). After proof aliunde of facts confessed.
- (5). Necessity and admissibility of entire statement.
- (6). Admissibility as affected by person to whom confession is made.

517.1.[61] Voluntary character of confession.
- (1). In general.
- (2). Necessity for showing voluntary character.
- (3). Exclusion if involuntary.

517.2 Absence or denial of counsel; inadequate representation.
- (1). In general.
- (2). Failure to request counsel; waiver.
- (3). Advising of right to counsel.

517.3 Proof of corpus delicti; corroboration in general.
- (1). In general.
- (2). Necessity of proof.
- (3). Requisites of proof.
- (4). Sufficiency in particular prosecutions.

518. Caution.
- (1). Necessity in general.
- (2). Necessity where accused is in custody.
- (3). Sufficiency.
- (4). Effect.

519. Voluntary character in general.
- (1). What confessions are voluntary.
- (2). Effect of prior involuntary confessions.
- (3). Confessions while in custody in general.
- (4). Confessions made to persons in authority.
- (5). Judicial confessions.
- (6). Confessions while in custody for other offense.

Table 3.2: Variables in the Involuntary Confession Cases[62]

Circumstances of Pressure:

1. Physical violence overtly designed to elicit a confession.
2. Physical violence *not* overtly designed to elicit a confession.
3. Nonviolent physical pressure, e.g., deprivation of food, sleep, or clothes, or long exposure to bright lights, etc., or any combination of these devices of pressure.
4. "Relay tactics" in questioning.
5. Protracted interrogation.
6. Verbal or mental coercion other than protracted interrogation, e.g., threat of physical violence, threat of arrest of relatives, statement by law-enforcing officers to the defendant that there is a threat of mob violence even though none actually might exist, false statement that accomplice has confessed, promise of leniency, or persuasion by a psychiatrist, or any combination of these devices of pressure.
7. Removal of the defendant to isolated places at night, for questioning.
8. Preceding admittedly coerced confession.
9. No other confession which is admittedly voluntary and indicative of the voluntary nature of the confession in question.
10. No formal presentation of charges.
11. Delay in the formal presentation of charges.
12. Detention incommunicado.
13. An actually existing threat of mob violence, which the defendant notes without being made aware of it by law-enforcing officers.
14. No advice of the right to remain silent.
15. No advice of the right to counsel.
16. Request of consultation with counsel denied.
17. No consultation with counsel prior to the confession.

Personal Circumstances Indicative of the Inability to Resist Pressure:

18. Negro status.
19. Youth and concomitant immaturity.

20. Illiteracy, subnormal education, ignorance of English, mental incapacity, or limited contact with the prevailing culture pattern. (Multiple values if more than one manifestation.)

21. No previous experience in criminal proceedings, or unfamiliarity with criminal procedure in spite of such previous experience.

Possible Modifying Circumstance:

22. No evidence which, apart from the challenged confession, would be sufficient for a conviction.

Table 3.3: Facts Used in Benesh Model

COERCIVE FORCES

1. Psychological coercion: Any threat or promise made, trickery, or deceit
2. Physical coercion: Any form of physical torture or beating, or the use of truth serums
3. Deprived of basic needs, including food or sleep
4. Length of detention
5. Place of detention
6. Had no attorney
7. Request or actual lawyer denied
8. Held incommunicado

POLICE PROCEDURE

9. *Miranda*: Before 1966 decision, this variable is coded as pertaining to "constitutional rights"
10. Right to remain silent
11. Right to have an attorney
12. Length of interrogation
13. Place of interrogation
14. Magistrate: Whether defendant brought before a judicial officer without unnecessary delay.
15. Police relays
16. Voluntary waiver: Whether defendant knowingly and intelligently waived his constitutional rights

DEFENDANT CHARACTERISTICS

17. Mental status of defendant
18. Intelligence of defendant
19. Race of defendant
20. Experience with legal system of defendant
21. Youth of defendant
22. Other characteristics impacting the admission of confession, such as drug addiction, motherhood, high blood pressure, illness, etc.

MITIGATING CIRCUMSTANCES

23. Mitigating circumstances: Factors serving to mitigate the involuntariness of confession, such as state v. federal issues, defendant studied criminal law, defendant being held for another crime during interrogation, etc.

COURTROOM PROCEDURE

24. Procedural fairness in determination of voluntariness

OTHER

25. Habeas corpus
26. Fruit of illegality: Confession fruit of either illegally obtained confession, illegal search and seizure, or illegal arrest U.S. detention
27. Harmless error

Table 3.4: Coding Rules

DECISION ON WHETHER TO CODE: Before delving into the coding scheme, do take note that not all cases in this defined universe were coded. IF THE CASE DOES NOT INVOLVE THE VOLUNTARINESS OF A CONFESSION, omit it. This need not be the sole issue, but it absolutely must be AT issue. If a confession is merely discussed but the appellant is not questioning its voluntary nature, I do not code the case. Common reasons not to code include corpus delecti questions, procedural issues (habeas corpus), admission of codefendant's confession against another, voluntariness of guilty pleas (but do code if they hinge on a coerced confession). Also, if a case doesn't have an adequate discussion of the facts at issue, do not code it. Make a quick note as to the reason for eliminating the case. If two codefendants are tried together, each alleging violations of their rights in the admission of a confession, code as two cases, noting the caseid for each. If the court quickly discards one of the claims, then just code it as one case. If a defendant makes several confessions, code only the one at issue. (Do note that later ones my be the fruits of earlier ones.)

Opinion Author = place a checkmark by the name of the judge writing the opinion. If the opinion is per curiam, note P.C. in the margin of the case.

vote = vote ON THE ADMISSIBILITY OF THE CONFESSION, as a whole number (e.g., 30 is a three to zero vote) Note: This is not always the same as the vote in the case.

judge1, judge2, judge3 = last names of judges. Add (dist.) if a district court judge, add (DC) if a DC judge is sitting by designation on the 2nd circuit for example, to denote a visiting judge. Add (sr.) if the justice is a senior judge sitting by designation. For en banc decisions, enter all the names, keeping the majority and minority together for easier coding. Note en banc in the margin, and I'd suggest reading these first to make sure they involve confession, because it is a difficult to list all the judges.

jvote1, jvote2, jvote3 = enter 1 for overturn confession, 0 for uphold. Overturn is used loosely, so if there is any indication that something is wrong or the case should be reheard or whatever, enter 1. 0 means the confession is acceptable as is and is without error.

confess = whether confession was upheld or not. Again, 1 for overturn, 0 for admit with rule as above.

party1,2,3...etc = party of judge measured as party of appointing president. 1=Democrat, 0=Republican. For Supreme Court, use Segal/Cover score.

enbanc = Circuit heard the case en banc. 1=en banc, 0=not.

percuriam = whether per curiam decision or not. 1=yes, 0=no.

denymag = whether accused was effectively denied the opportunity to see a magistrate (e.g., there were no mitigating circumstances). 1=was denied, 0=was not denied.

disposit = disposition of lower court decision: A = affirmed, R=remanded, Rev=reversed, M=modified, V=vacated, plus any combination thereof.

psych = whether psychological coercion is present. This includes threats, promises, and any other form of inducement which is not physical and is discussed as such by the court. 2=there was psychological coercion, 1=there was no psych coercion, 0=not mentioned at all.

phys = whether physical coercion is present. This is beatings and the like referred to by the Court as physically obtaining a confession. 2=was physical coercion, 1=was no physical coercion, 0=not mentioned.

len_det = whether length of the detention was mentioned as contributing to the involuntariness of the confession. 2=held for an unreasonable length of time, 1=was not held long, 0=not mentioned

pl_deten = whether the place of detention was such that it provided a coercive atmosphere 2=held in a bad place, 1=facilities were fine, 0=not mentioned.

nomagis = whether defendant was brought before a committing magistrate before s/he confessed. 2=was NOT brought before the magistrate, 1=was brought before magistrate, 0=not mentioned. Note: When the court decides that the defendant did confess before being brought before a judicial officer, but that the delay in such bringing was not unnecessary, add a mitigating factor "not unnecessary" but still mark nomagis as 2.

nomirand = for cases arising after Miranda and subject to it, code whether appropriate warnings were given. 2=warnings NOT given, 1=appropriate warnings given, 0=not mentioned or not applicable.

nosilent = before or after Miranda, whether suspect was informed of his right to remain silent. 2=was NOT warned of this right, 1=was warned, 0=not mentioned.

noatty = before or after Miranda, whether suspect was informed of his right to have an attorney. 2=was NOT warned of this right, 1=was warned, 0=not mentioned. Note: Only after Miranda do suspects have to be told that they can have an atty during interrogation and that if they cannot afford an atty one will be appointed for them. If this extra warning is at issue, but the police did tell the accused he had the right to an atty, mark noatty 1 and nomirand 2.

codef = whether the accused codefendant's confession was admitted at the trial. 2=codefendant's confession admitted, 1=codefendant's confession not admitted, 0=not mentioned.

mental = whether the accused has a mental deficiency (retardation, brain damage, insanity). 2=has a mental problem, 1=no mental deficiency, 0=not mentioned.

intell = whether the accused is intelligent. 2=is intelligent, 1=not intelligent (moron status, etc.), 0=not mentioned.

race = whether it is mentioned that the accused belongs to ANY minority race. 2=minority, 1=not minority, 0=not mentioned. Note: Generally, only the presence of this matters, so choices are really 2 or 0 here.

hasexper = whether accused has ANY experience with the law. 2=has experience, 1=does not have experience, 0=not mentioned.

youth = whether accused is young or not (and the court mentions that he's young — generally 18 or younger). 2=is young, 1=is not a youth, 0=not mentioned.

other = any other characteristic that the accused possesses which hinges on the voluntariness of his confession (drug addiction, drunk during questioning, sick, tired, etc.). 2=is another characteristic (write it in), 1=is not other characteristic (write it in -- e.g., the accused was not drunk), 0=not mentioned.

mitigate = whether any mitigating circumstance existed so that the accused confession could be called voluntary. For example, the delay in bringing before a magistrate was not unnecessary; or the accused was in custody for another crime; or this was a state not a federal arrest (so McNabb doesn't apply); or the questioner wasn't a police officer. 2=mitigating circumstance exists (write it in), 1=mitigating did not exist (write it in — not very common at all), 0=not mentioned.

waiver = accused made a knowing and intelligent waiver of his rights (atty and silence). 2=made waiver, 1=did not waive (or did not do so intelligently), 0=not mentioned.

procedur = whether the procedure for determining voluntariness by thc trial court was adequate; that is, was the accused afforded a separate hearing outside the presence of the jury and then was the confession admitted to it (as per Jackson v. Denno). 2=procedure was FAULTY, 1=procedure was fine, 0=not mentioned.

volun = whether or not the accused volunteered the information taken before being asked any questions. 2=volunteered info, 1=did not volunteer info, 0=not mentioned.

unrep = whether or not the accused had an attorney, but code only if the court mentions this explicitly. 2=had NO attorney, 1=had an attorney with him, 0=not mentioned.

len_int = whether the confession was tainted due to the length of the interrogation. 2=long interrogation, 1=interrogation of reasonable length, 0=not mentioned.

relays = whether the police interrogated the suspect using relays of officers (the court will call it thus). 2=relays were employed, 1=no relays, 0=not mentioned.

incommun = whether the accused was held incommunicado, that is, without access to friends, family, attorney, etc. In the company of police officers only. 2=held incommunicado, 1=not held incommunicado (was allowed to call mother, see sister, etc), 0=not mentioned.

habeas = whether this appeal is on habeas corpus. 2=habeas, 0=not.

harmless = whether the error involved was deemed by the court to have been harmless. 2=harmless, 1=not harmless, 0=not mentioned.

factdis = whether there was a factual dispute among the judges on the panel. These can arise in concurrences or dissents. 2=factual disagreement, 0=none.

pl_int = whether the place of interrogation contributed to the involuntariness of the confession. 2=bad place where the suspect was interrogated, 1=place was fine, 0=not mentioned.

depbasic = whether the accused was deprived of basic needs during questioning, like sleep, food, clothes, etc. 2=deprived of basic human needs, 1=not deprived, 0=not mentioned.

priorcc = whether there was a prior coerced confession which may have tainted the one under attack. 2=there was a prior coerced confession, 1=there was no prior confession, 0=not mentioned.

fruit = whether the confession was the fruit of some illegality, like illegal arrest, illegal search and seizure, illegal detention, etc. 2=was the fruit, 1=was not the fruit, 0=not mentioned.

req_atty = whether the accused requested and was refused an attorney. 2=did request/was refused, 1=did not request, or requested and was not refused, 0=not mentioned.

CHAPTER 4

Decision Making in the United States Courts of Appeals

In order to test the theory about principal agency and the relevance of all four models of judicial decision making, several models of Courts of Appeals decision making are constructed and tested using the universe of confession cases for the time period 1946 – 1981. As a measure of the legal, and, to some extent, institutional model, Supreme Court precedent is included, measured by way of relevant facts coded for their applicability. This is an innovative use of fact pattern analysis (FPA) as applied to this hierarchical relationship. As mentioned in Chapter 3, I argue that FPA measures the influence of precedent, with each fact a proxy for the holding of the precedent in question. This provides a test of the legal model as precedential considerations loom large there, and a test of the neo-institutional model as the hierarchical environment of the Courts of Appeals is highlighted in their attention to the higher court. In order to test the attitudinal model, I include measures of "liberalness" of the Courts of Appeals, using party as a proxy (this is discussed further below). Finally, I test the strategic, and, indirectly, the neo-institutional model, by including a measure of Supreme Court ideology. Because the potential for Supreme Court supervision always exists, the lower court will also look at the ideological composition of the High Court and consider that majority's ideological bent in reaching its own decision, possibly in attempts to predict what the Supreme Court would do should it choose to hear an appeal of the case now before the Court of Appeals. This would be considered strategic behavior because the lower court, if it should so behave, would look forward to potential Supreme Court action when making its decision, thereby considering its principal in making its choice. In addition, this serves as an institutional constraint, highlighting the lower court's inferior position and attention to the Supreme Court.[63]

We must recognize, before going further, that these two courts are not hearing the same kinds of cases and so, we would not expect every fact relevant to Supreme Court decisions to be influential at the Courts of Appeals because they simply may not get cases containing certain facts. Indeed, simple frequencies run on the individual facts do indicate that the Supreme Court takes cases with quantitatively more facts present; that is, the cases heard by the Supreme Court have, as present, a whole host of factual considerations (see Table 4.1). High percentages of Supreme Court cases include psychological coercion, for example (32%). However, in the Courts of Appeals, only 6% of the cases contain psychological coercion (see Table 4.2). However, this problem is mitigated in part by the coding scheme employed. As discussed in Chapter 3, I coded both for the presence and absence of certain facts. As can be seen in Tables 4.1 and 4.2, the mention of a fact in any way (either by way of noting its absence or presence) is quite similar across the two levels of courts. Indeed, the Courts of Appeals may be presented with less meritorious cases in that they contain none of the problems noted as reversible error by the Supreme Court. However, the Courts of Appeals still note their absence and we can assume that, at times, the absence of a particular egregious error in the handling of a confession may be as important as the presence of such an error. Both the presence and absence of particular facts are considered for inclusion into the model. The lack of the presence of facts though, does provide good reason why the Courts of Appeals should affirm more confessions. Indeed, examining the dependent variable under study here, we find that while the Supreme Court overturns 68% of the confessions it reviews, the Courts of Appeals overturn only 22%. That the two courts differ in their resolution of these cases, however, does not preclude a finding of attention to Supreme Court precedent, and whether the Courts of Appeals heed the Supreme Court is the most important question here under study. It may indicate, though, that the opportunity for influence may be depressed because of the cases the Courts of Appeals hear.

I also explore the possibility that the twelve circuits of the U.S. Courts of Appeals differ one from another via the inclusion of a dummy variable for each circuit, for the purpose of attempting to determine whether justice in this area of the law is determined, at least partially, by which circuit heard the case, or, alternatively, whether all the circuits are deciding cases compatibly, thereby contributing to "equal justice." If a difference among circuits is discovered, that difference will need to be explained either with reference to the cases decided by the unique circuit(s), by reference to its differential ideological makeup, or via an explanation of the unique decision-making process employed by that specific circuit.[64]

4.1 The Supreme Court in Confession Cases

A major consideration in this chapter is the facts that the Courts of Appeals should arguably be attentive to in deciding confession cases. In order to identify said facts it is necessary to carefully assess the Supreme Court's jurisprudence in this area of the law. The lower courts, after all, can only apply a given fact to their analyses once that fact is identified as "mattering" to the determination of voluntariness.[65] As was discussed in Chapter 3 and in the previous section, the Supreme Court has decided confession cases in an incremental fashion. In other words, it made no sweeping conclusions about what types of, and under what circumstances, confessions should be allowed. Rather, it took cases in which a seeming injustice occurred and noted that certain facts in that lower court decision contributed to its determination. Because no constitutional language explicitly addresses coerced confessions, the Court was forced to deal with each circumstance as it arose. First, the Court focused on the "third degree" tactics employed by police departments, finding that any confession obtained via physical coercion could not stand (*Brown v. Mississippi* 297 U.S. 278 (1936)). However, in that same case, the Court extended coercion to include threats and other psychological measures. The Court also discussed the need for judicial advice before an accused is interrogated (*McNabb v. U.S.* 318 U.S. 332 (1943)), and, using the Fourth Amendment (*Silverthorne Lumber Co. v. U.S.* 251 U.S. 385 (1920)), recognized the inherent danger in using an arguably voluntary confession when said confession was preceded by a decidedly involuntary one. The Court also recognized that the amount of coercion in the case must be relative to the suspect's ability to withstand the pressure (*Chambers v. Florida* 309 U.S. 227 (1940)). In *Chambers,* the Court opened the door to consider any range of characteristics of the accused that might mitigate or aggravate the finding of voluntariness. All of these facts were established as material by the Court prior to the start of my analysis (1946) and so are expected to influence the decision making of the Courts of Appeals throughout the period under study.

During the period being analyzed, the Court decided other precedent-setting cases. These include *Wong Sun v. U.S.* (371 U.S. 471 (1963)), which excluded confessions obtained as a result of a prior illegality (a prior invalid search or an invalid arrest, etc); *Townsend v. Sain* and *Jackson v. Denno* (372 U.S. 293 (1963) and 378 U.S. 368 (1964) respectively), which established standards for the determination of voluntariness; *Lynumn v. Illinois* (372 U.S. 528 (1963)), which rendered inapplicable harmless error analysis to confessions; *Escobedo v. Illinois* (378 U.S. 478 (1964)), which held that once an accused requests counsel all interrogation must cease; *Miranda v. Arizona* (384 U.S. 436 (1966)), which delineated the warnings that must be given upon arrest in order to deem a confession voluntary; *Bruton v. U.S.* (391 U.S. 123 (1968)), which precluded use of a codefendant's confession against another codefendant; and *Milton v. Wainwright* (407 U.S. 371 (1972)), which did use harmless error analysis to uphold a conviction based upon a confession.

The Court obviously decided other cases during this time as well, but most involved certain *combinations* of fact that lead either to upholding or reversing the use of a confession, and therefore did not present the lower court with any new precedent, as such, to apply. In other words, the Supreme Court, once it announced its determination of the facts to be considered in the voluntariness calculation, then took cases that had certain combinations of fact, perhaps to confirm that those factors rendered a confession involuntary (in most cases). It may well be, however, that the reaffirmation of certain facts by the Supreme Court will lead the Courts of Appeals to more fully comply. Such facts would include the Miranda warnings, the prohibition of physical or psychological coercion, and some defendant characteristics. From the earlier mentioned frequencies, we can glean some expectations about which facts will be most important to the Courts of Appeals. As seen in

Table 4.1, the most important facts should be the warnings about Constitutional protections (and Miranda), psychological coercion, length of interrogation, incommunicado detention, and magistrate presentation. These represent repeated instructions by the Court regarding the handling of these confession cases. It seems reasonable that the Courts of Appeals may pay more heed to those factors repeatedly treated by the Supreme Court (provided, of course, that the High Court is consistent in its treatment), and so I discuss that contention here as well, calling it the "differential strength" hypothesis.

Each of the aforementioned circumstances, then, is included in a fact-based (i.e., precedent-based) model of Courts of Appeals decision making. For precedents decided before 1946, the facts themselves are included, as they should have been germane to the Courts of Appeals for the entire period under study. For those decided after that date, however, a dummy variable is created for the applicability of the precedent which encompasses the period from the year in which the case was decided to the present[66] and is interacted with the relevant fact. These are then entered into the equation. It is assumed that the given facts will not matter to the Courts of Appeals before the Supreme Court decided the applicable case, but that assumption will be tested as well.

4.2 Decision Making on the Courts of Appeals

The following model (Equation 4-1) was tested on the Courts of Appeals data:

$$P(Y_i = 1) = F(\beta_1\ \textit{reqatty*Escobedo} - \beta_2\ \textit{noreq} * \textit{Escobedo} - \beta_3\ \textit{nofruit} * \textit{WongSun} + \beta_4\ \textit{fruit} * \textit{WongSun} + \beta_5\ \textit{procedure} * \textit{Townsend} - \beta_6\ \textit{noprocedure} * \textit{Townsend} + \beta_7\ \textit{codef} * \textit{Bruton} - \beta_8\ \textit{miranda*Miranda} + \beta_9\ \textit{nomiranda} * \textit{Miranda} - \beta_{10}\ \textit{magistrate} * \textit{Mallory} + \beta_{11}\ \textit{nomagis} * \textit{Mallory} - \beta_{12}\ \textit{waiver} * \textit{Miranda} + \beta_{13}\ \textit{nowaiver} * \textit{Miranda} + \beta_{14}\ \textit{psych} - \beta_{15}\ \textit{nopsych} - \beta_{16}\ \textit{volun} + \beta_{17}\ \textit{novolun} + \beta_{18}\ \textit{priorcc} + \beta_{19}\ \textit{pldeten} + \beta_{20}\ \textit{race} + \beta_{21}\ \textit{other} - \beta_{22}\ \textit{noother} + \beta_{23}\ \textit{incomm} - \beta_{24}\ \textit{noincomm} - \beta_{25}\ \textit{hasexper} + \beta_{26}\ \textit{noexper} + \beta_{27}\ \textit{youth} - \beta_{28}\ \textit{noyouth} + \beta_{29}\ \textit{deprive} - \beta_{30}\ \textit{nodeprive} + \beta_{31}\ \textit{ideol} +$$

β_{32} ***highct*** + β_{33} ***lowercourt*** – β_{34} ***habeas*** + β_{35} ***enbanc*** + ε) **[4-1]**[67]

where ***reqatty* * *Escobedo*** indicates that an accused requested and was denied an attorney after the Supreme Court's decision in Escobedo; ***noreq* * *Escobedo*** indicates that the accused either did not request an attorney or was not denied one after Escobedo was decided; ***nofruit* * *WongSun*** takes a value of one when the confession at issue was not the fruit of some illegality after the Court's decision in Wong Sun; ***fruit* * *WongSun*** takes a value of one when there was some illegality found to have induced a coerced confession; ***procedure* * *Townsend*** indicates a problem with the procedure in a trial heard after Townsend; ***noproc* * *Townsend*** indicates a fair proceeding; ***codef* * *Bruton*** indicates that a codefendant's confession was introduced against the defendant after the Supreme Court heard Bruton; ***miranda* * *Miranda*** is one when the accused was given the Miranda warnings after the High Court's decision in that case; ***nomiranda* * *Miranda*** flags those cases in which warnings were not given; ***magistrate* * *Mallory*** indicates that the accused was brought before a magistrate after the Court's decision in Mallory; ***nomagis* * *Mallory*** indicates some delay in bringing the accused before a magistrate; ***waiver* * *Miranda*** indicates that the Court found there to exist a knowing and intelligent waiver of the defendant's rights; ***nowaiver* * *Miranda*** indicates that there was no waiver; ***psych*** measures the presence of psychological coercion; ***nopsych*** measures the absence of such psychological coercion; ***volun*** is equal to one when the accused volunteered the statements under consideration; ***novolun*** is one when the accused did not volunteer the statements; ***priorcc*** is present when an accused made a previous coerced confession prior to the one at issue; ***pldeten*** indicates that the accused is being held in a coercive atmosphere; ***race*** is a dummy denoting any minority status of the accused; ***other*** takes a value of one when there is some other characteristic of the defendant that contributes to pressure being brought to bear; ***noother*** measures the absence of such characteristics; ***incomm*** denotes incommunicado detention where the accused is denied the opportunity to speak with friends, family, or counsel; ***noincomm*** signifies the absence of such detention; ***hasexper*** is equal to one for those defendants having experience with the law or the criminal justice system; ***noexper*** notes those defendants without such experience; ***youth*** indicates the accused is less than 18; ***noyouth*** indicates the accused is not younger than 18; ***deprive*** denotes the deprivation of basic needs such as water, food, or clothing; ***nodep*** indicates the accused was deprived of none of these; ***ideol*** is the "liberalness" of the Courts of Appeals panel; ***highct*** is the "liberalness" of the Supreme Court; ***lowerco*** is the resolution of the case in the trial court; ***habeas*** is a dummy indicating a habeas corpus petition; and ***enbanc*** is a dummy indicating that the circuit heard the case en banc. The expected direction of each is indicated by its contribution to or detraction from the likelihood of a confession's exclusion. I assume that cases heard en banc are more likely to be reversed (extending Supreme Court treatment logic – that they hear them to reverse them) and that confessions appealed on habeas are less likely to be excluded because these are more likely to be frivolous. All others should be self-evident from the discussion in the previous chapter.

4.3 Coding of the Variables

Although I have previously discussed the coding of many of the variables (i.e., those based on facts in the opinion), there are a few that warrant further consideration. These include ***ideol*** and ***highct***.

Ideology has been assumed to be an important consideration in judicial decision making for some time, but the measurement of attitudes is something not so widely agreed upon. In the Supreme Court, because we know the justices well, we can use scaling techniques and past voting to predict future decision making. However, we are just beginning to study the Courts of Appeals, so there is much more uncertainty. In addition, the large number of judges precludes careful examination and scaling of each individually. I assume that once we "get to know" those judges better, we will begin to be able to predict their decision making, at least to the extent that ideology is found to matter by use of some of these scaling techniques. However, until then, I think a different measure is needed. Therefore, as my measure of ideology, I use the party of the appointing president, assuming Democratic appointees tend to be more liberal and Republican appointees more conservative. I then create an ideology score for each panel, which is the percentage of liberal judges on the panel. I expect ideology to be positive, as liberal panels will more likely exclude a confession.

There are other measures of ideology one could employ, however, and these should at least be discussed. First, I could use the ADA scores of the appointing president in combination with the ADA scores of the senators in the state from which the judge is appointed as Giles, Hettinger, and Peppers (1998) do. However, as they themselves admit, party does just as well in civil liberties cases. Because I am dealing with that sort of issue area, using party seems justified.

I also considered the PAJID measure created by Brace, Langer and Hall (1998) for use in the states, but I think it neither possible nor efficient to measure these federal judges in this manner. True, I could use the public mood of the state from which these judges are being appointed assuming the senators from that state heed public mood, but that begs the question of whether it is the senator or the president which has more influence over these appointments. If it is the senator, surely we could use the PAJID measure. If it is the president, however, and I contend that it is especially at this lower federal court level, I would be hesitant to use a public mood sort of formulation to measure ideology for the appeals court judges. Using public mood as part of an ideological measure for judges also implies that the public matters to these judges. While there is some evidence of this at the state court level, there is very little at the Courts of Appeals level. It seems more defensible to rely upon the ideology of the appointing president, assuming, as many scholars have found, that presidents do attempt to appoint like-minded judges to the federal bench. Surely this measure is not perfect as Democratic presidents vary among themselves as to their degree of liberalism, but it seems to be the best measure available.

One study provides some indication that using party affiliation is not such a bad choice. In a meta-analysis of 140 books, articles, dissertations, and conference papers to examine whether there is a link between political party affiliation and judicial ideology, Pinello (1999) finds that indeed there is and, therefore, any more complicated measures lack efficiency. Therefore, I employ the party of the judge (here, measured as the party of the appointing president) as my ideology measure.

To measure High Court ideology, I use the Segal/Cover scores in a yearly average. Segal and Cover, using content analytic techniques, "derive independent and reliable measures of the values of all Supreme Court justices from Earl Warren to Anthony Kennedy" (1989:557). Segal, Epstein, Cameron and Spaeth (1995) update, backdate, and extend the Segal and Cover analysis to include the two Bush appointees, and the seven Roosevelt and four Truman nominees. We therefore have a score for every justice on the Vinson, Warren and Burger Courts, which are under study in this analysis. By adding the scores of the nine sitting justices in a given term and dividing by nine, we can obtain a yearly score. Using that yearly score, I score each term of the Court as either "liberal" or "conservative."[68] This measure is admittedly gross, but is superior to any annually fluctuating alternative because it does not rely on votes. This variable should also be positive, as the more liberal the High Court, the more likely the Courts of Appeals should be to overturn a confession, fearing that if it decides otherwise it will be overturned upon review.

With these measures in mind, we turn to the results.

4.4 Results

The results of the first estimation are contained in Table 4.3.[69] Do note that I've estimated this model using robust standard errors. The reason for this is that any multiple regression technique assumes the independence of observations, and usually this is not a problem. Here, however, since I have multiple observations from the same circuit and even the same panel, any contention that they are strictly independent is dubious at best. The estimation of robust standard errors corrects for this and produces more plausible results. Looking then at the model, we are immediately impressed with the fit. (See note 75 for model fit statistics). The pseudo R^2 is an impressive 0.71, although we should take care not to garner too much satisfaction from this fact, given the problems with R^2 measures in general and the pseudo-R^2 specifically.[70] In addition to this evidence of goodness of fit, we also find that the model predicts an impressive 94% of all cases correctly, which translates into a substantial 73% reduction in error over the null model.

There is much of interest in these results. First, nearly all variables are in the expected direction, and most are significant. However, the model is certainly not perfect, as expected, and so some variables are incorrectly signed and/or insignificant. The variables with incorrect signs are ***magis * Mallory*** and ***habeas*** both of which are also insignificant, and ***pldeten*** which is negatively related to the exclusion of a confession for some curious reason. Insignificant variables include ***noproc * Townsend***, ***miranda * Miranda***, ***waiver * Miranda***, ***hasexper***, ***youth***, and ***deprive***. It is interesting to note, however, that the absence of all of the insignificant variables (save habeas) does contribute to the decision making of the Courts of Appeals in this area of the law. Indeed, the failure to present the accused before a magistrate, a problematic procedure, the absence of Miranda warnings and of a rights waiver all contribute to a finding of involuntariness. Similarly, the absence of youth, deprivation of needs, and experience with the law all impact the confession decision. Therefore, our insignificant findings do not impact our substantive conclusions at all. Indeed, these precedents of the Supreme Court are relevant.

The clear majority of the variables are both correctly signed and statistically significant, however. Requests for attorneys and their absence are both significant influences on the determination of voluntariness. Whether or not the confession was a fruit of a prior illegality is also influential, with the presence increasing the probability of exclusion and the absence attenuating it. Both the presence of psychological coercion and its absence produce a statistically significant influence on the exclusion of a confession, with its presence adding to the probability of exclusion, and absence decreasing that contingency. This was a fact in many of the Supreme Court precedents, and so our "differential strength" hypothesis receives some validation. Volunteered information from the defendant detracts from confession exclusion, and the absence of such volunteered information increases the likelihood of exclusion. The existence of a prior coerced confession adds to the probability that a later confession will be excluded, as do several characteristics of the accused come including race, other characteristics broadly defined, inexperience with the law, and age. The Courts of Appeals are far more likely to rule as the lower court did, evidenced by the significant and positive coefficient on that variable, and they do pay some heed to the ideological composition of the Supreme Court, as that variable is positive and significant. Finally, en banc decisions do tend to exclude confessions more often than single panel decisions do.

It is interesting to note the differential success of the more recently established precedents. Obviously the Courts of Appeals pay heed to a number of old precedents, evidenced both by those facts authoritatively established prior to the beginning of this analysis that are significant in the model and those other facts that, because of perfect prediction, could not be included (bearing on such precedents as *Chambers v. Florida* (race), *Lisenba v. California* 314 U.S. 219 (1941) (relays)). However, the Courts of Appeals do not seem to heed all of the High Court's pronouncements. We see here that *Wong Sun*, *Townsend*, *Escobedo* and *Miranda* are all significantly related to the lower court's determination of voluntariness, while *Bruton* and *Mallory* were not. Neither are those Supreme Court precedents that deal with intelligence of defendant, lack of representation, length of interrogation, and place of interrogation. For many of the variables, however, a mere lack of frequency that explains their insignificance. Exploration into why this is so for those where there are enough instances of fact presence will flow from the analysis in Chapter 5, where I specifically test Courts of Appeals' compliance with specific precedents, attempting to explain differential compliance as a function of characteristics of the Supreme Court cases themselves and ideological interagreement between the Supreme Court and the deciding panel.[71]

Finally, ideology is significant, as expected, and decidedly so. Even though I measure this variable somewhat grossly, as discussed earlier, it is significant at the 0.002 level. And its impact on the probability of exclusion is far from negligible as well. Liberal panels are substantially more likely to exclude a confession than are conservative ones. A change from a one-liberal panel (ideology=0.33) to a two-liberal panel (ideology=0.67) increases the likelihood of exclusion, when all other variables are held at their means, from 3.3% to 7.1%. When there are no liberals on the panel, only 1.4% of confessions are excluded. When liberals fill the panel, the likelihood of exclusion is 13.3%. Surely this is a substantial influence. This demonstrates that while the Courts of Appeals judges do pay heed to the precedents of the Supreme Court, at least in their realization as case facts, they remain consistent with their own ideology, notwithstanding the indirect way in which I measure it.

In addition to mentioning their significance or insignificance, we may also discuss the differential influence of Supreme Court precedents on the exclusion of a confession as we did for ideology. Table 4.4

displays predicted probabilities of exclusion for the minimum and maximum value of each variable in the model. From this table, we see that *Wong Sun*, or that the confession is the fruit of an illegality, generates the greatest impact on the decision to exclude the confession, with its presence increasing the probability that the panel will rule against the admission by 84.4%, *ceteris paribus*. Lack of a waiver is also quite influential, with its presence making the likelihood of exclusion 75.5% (up from 5.2% when all variables are at their respective means). The least influential variable is the insignificant habeas corpus indicator, which only increases the likelihood of exclusion, when present, 0.2%. The variables we expected to be disproportionately influential, at least according to the sheer number of Supreme Court treatments thereof, are indeed highly influential (psychological coercion, lack of *Miranda* warnings, incommunicado detention, and denial of presentation before a magistrate). This makes good sense.

4.5 Differences Among Circuits

We found before beginning this analysis that the variation across circuits with respect to the mean proportion of liberal decisions rendered each year does not show differences substantial enough to render the circuits incomparable. (See note 64.) However, we might still wonder whether any of the circuits follow different decisional processes in these cases. Indeed, can we talk about "the Court of Appeals" as an institution, or must we understand this federal appellate court to be twelve circuit "Courts of Appeals?" In order to determine to what extent the Courts of Appeals decide cases in accord with one another, I conducted a couple of simple analyses. First, I ran the model [4-1] that fits the Courts of Appeals generally, with a dummy variable for each specific circuit individually. That is, I ran one model with a dummy for the DC circuit, one with a dummy for the First circuit, and so on. In so doing, only the DC and tenth circuits differed significantly, evidenced by the significance of the coefficient on those dummy.[72] To explore this difference, I ran another model in which all of the dummy variables for circuit were included, excepting the DC circuit which was used as the baseline (meaning that each dummy can be interpreted as first circuit or DC circuit, second circuit or DC circuit, etc.). As can be seen from Table 4.5, all of the circuits significantly deviate from the DC circuit, and most are less likely to exclude a confession than that circuit. This is interesting, as we find that one circuit court is seemingly behaving more like the Supreme Court than are the others, although its frequency of overturning a confession (it does so 45% of the time – see Table 4.7) still pales in comparison with the High Court's. The same analysis was conducted using the tenth circuit as the baseline and those results are presented in Table 4.6 Again, all of the circuits are significantly different from the tenth, but here, all are more likely to exclude a confession. Table 4.7 displays the circuit courts' frequency of overturning confessions, showing explicitly the much lower rate at which the 10th Circuit excludes confessions. Its lack of exclusions and the DC Circuits' plethora of them stand out from a listing of otherwise similar exclusion rates. In order to determine whether these differences might be ideological in nature, Table 4.8 was constructed. There, we see few major differences, although the DC Circuit is the second most liberal. However, the 10th Circuit, significantly less likely to exclude a confession, has a mean ideology of 0.61; just 0.05 less than the DC Circuit. Ideology probably cannot explain the differences we find here.

Overall, we do find substantial evidence that the lower court considers the Supreme Court in making its decision in this area of law; and they do so across the board. No circuit ignores Supreme Court prescription. While the D.C. and Tenth Circuits are somewhat anomalous, both still heed Supreme Court precedent and consider Supreme Court ideology. This finding, our most important, indicates that the Courts of Appeals and the Supreme Court do exist in some sort of hierarchical relationship.

4.6 Conclusions

Through these analyses, we have found that all four models of Supreme Court decision making have some bearing on decision making in the Courts of Appeals. Our formulation of principal-agent theory, which includes attitudes, law, strategy, and institutions, is useful in understanding Courts of Appeals decision making. The lower court is affected by its attitudes; liberal panels are more likely to exclude confessions. The Courts of Appeals are influenced by legal considerations; many of the Supreme Court's factual considerations are given considerable weight by the Courts of Appeals. While adherence to Supreme Court precedent could be categorized as a legal consideration (the influence of precedent), we might also use the success of that set of variables to argue that the Courts of Appeals is indeed constrained by its institutional position in the judicial hierarchy. That they probably pay heed to the ideological makeup of the Supreme Court lends additional credence to that model, and as well provides some fodder for the relevance of the strategic model, as judges look forward to a Supreme Court decision on the merits and decide their case, at least in part, in order to avoid reversal.

In addition, I find that the various circuits of the Courts of Appeals do not much differ from one another, although the D.C. and 10th Circuits are clearly different. In the case of the D.C. Circuit, these differences may be due to the different types of cases that circuit hears, or its jurisdiction over the District of Columbia. Probably it differs because it need not deal with state habeas corpus cases which are more likely to contain frivolous appeals. In terms of the 10th Circuit, perhaps its carving from the 9th Circuit begat a different set of institutional norms. Or perhaps it behaves differently because of the large number of criminal appeals it hears, second only to the number heard by the Eleventh Circuit as a proportion of its docket (Songer, Sheehan and Haire 2001). Either way, we can be comforted that generally it matters not which circuit hears a case; even the outliers heed Supreme Court precedent. Overall, the lower court is constrained by precedent, by the Supreme Court, and by its hierarchical position. These differential constraints cause it to decide cases differently from the High Court. But by no means are they completely free agents.

Table 4.1: Number of Cases Mentioning Confession Facts
The Supreme Court

Fact	Total Mentions (Present or Absent)	%	Fact Present	%
Silence Warning	32	56	19	33
Attorney Warning	32	56	19	33
Psychological	28	49	18	32
Miranda Warnings	27	47	17	30
Length Interrogation	25	44	18	32
Incommunicado	23	40	20	35
Magistrate Hearing	19	33	16	28
Intelligence	17	30	14	25
Procedural Fairness	17	30	7	12
Request for Attorney	17	30	13	23
Had No Attorney	16	28	13	23
Deprived of Basic	16	28	9	16
Police Relays	15	26	13	23
Physical Coercion	14	25	3	5
Minority Race	14	25	14	25
Mental	11	19	9	16
Experience With Law	11	19	4	7
Length of Detention	10	18	9	16
Mitigating	10	18	10	18
Youth	9	16	5	9
Other Characteristics	9	16	10	18
Fruit of Illegality	7	12	5	9
Prior Coerced	6	11	5	9
Place of Detention	5	9	5	9
Waiver of Miranda	4	7	0	0
Volunteered	4	7	2	4
Harmless Error	4	7	3	5
Codefendant Confess	3	5	3	5
Place of Interrogation	3	5	3	5

Total Mentions = 408 Facts Per Case = 7
Total Present = 286 Facts Per Case = 5

Table 4.2: Number of Cases Mentioning Confession Facts
The Courts of Appeals

Fact	Total Mentions (Present or Absent)	%	Fact Present	%
Silence Warning	480	72	75	11
Attorney Warning	453	68	90	14
Miranda Warnings	302	45	33	5
Psychological	284	43	37	6
Magistrate Hearing	260	39	195	29
Procedural Fairness	253	38	206	31
Physical Coercion	187	28	4	1
Waiver of Miranda	178	27	154	23
Request for Attorney	133	20	30	5
Had No Attorney	110	16	86	13
Fruit of Illegality	106	16	28	4
Other Characteristics	96	14	50	8
Length of	95	14	23	3
Intelligence	82	12	34	5
Volunteered	82	12	78	12
Incommunicado	77	12	37	6
Deprived of Basic	75	11	17	3
Youth	64	10	41	6
Mental	50	7	27	4
Experience With Law	47	7	36	5
Minority Race	34	5	33	5
Length of Detention	30	4	17	3
Prior Coerced	29	4	18	3
Harmless Error	28	4	15	2
Police Relays	23	3	16	2
Codefendant	16	2	14	2
Place of Detention	11	2	8	1
Place of Interrogation	8	1	2	<1

Total Mentions = 3797 Facts Per Case = 5.7
Total Present = 1404 Present Per Case = 2

Table 4.3: Model of Courts of Appeals Decision Making[73]

Independent Variable	Coefficient (r.s.e.)	Sig Level
Request Atty * Escobedo	1.29 (.63)	0.039
No Request * Escobedo	-0.75 (.35)	0.031
No Fruit * Wong Sun	-0.94 (.42)	0.024
Fruit * Wong Sun	2.97 (.55)	0.000
Procedure * Townsend	1.85 (.34)	0.000
No Procedure * Townsend	-0.2 (.27)	0.460
Codefendent * Bruton	0.14 (.56)	0.798
Miranda Warnings * Miranda	-0.15 (.31)	0.632
No Warnings * Miranda	1.14 (.36)	0.002
Magistrate * Mallory	0.2 (.39)	0.605
No Magistrate * Mallory	0.47 (25)	0.057
Waiver * Miranda	-0.67 (.44)	0.132
No Waiver * Miranda	2.41 (.59)	0.000
Psychological Coercion	2.23 (.48)	0.000
No Psychological Coercion	-0.59 (.24)	0.014
Volunteered Statement	-1.53 (.51)	0.003
No Volunteered Statement	1.18 (.45)	0.009
Prior Coerced Confession	1.71 (.49)	0.001
Place of Detention	-1.83 (.73)	0.013
Race	0.97 (.52)	0.062
Other Characteristic of Acc	1.07 (.30)	0.000
No Other Characteristics	-1.07 (.28)	0.026
Held Incommunicado	1.65 (.49)	0.001
No Incommunicado	-1.06 (.71)	0.134
Has Experience With Law	-0.201 (.49)	0.683
No Experience With Law	2.37 (.93)	0.011
Is a Youth	0.34 (.45)	0.448
Not a Youth	-2.61 (1.07)	0.014
Deprivation of Needs	1.57 (1.00)	0.117
No Deprivation of Needs	-1.07 (.47)	0.022
Ideology of CA Panel	1.09 (.35)	0.002
High Court Ideology	0.46 (.23)	0.044
Lower Court Disposition	1.38 (.22)	0.000
Habeas Corpus Claim	0.02 (.21)	0.927
Heard En Banc	1.11 (.53)	0.037
Constant	-2.55 (.39)	0.000

Table 4.4: Marginal Effects of Independent Variables

Independent Variable	Pred Prob Min[74]	Pred Prob Max
Request Atty * Escobedo	0.047	0.350
No Request * Escobedo	0.064	0.011
No Fruit * Wong Sun	0.063	0.007
Fruit * Wong Sun	0.043	0.896
Procedure * Townsend	0.041	0.546
No Procedure * Townsend	0.058	0.038
Codefendent * Bruton	0.052	0.069
Miranda Warnings * Miranda	0.059	0.043
No Warnings * Miranda	0.046	0.294
Magistrate * Mallory	0.050	0.075
No Magistrate * Mallory	0.040	0.101
Waiver * Miranda	0.075	0.017
No Waiver * Miranda	0.043	0.755
Psychological Coercion	0.039	0.682
No Psychological Coercion	0.080	0.023
Volunteered Statement	0.075	0.001
No Volunteered Statement	0.051	0.325
Prior Coerced Confession	0.047	0.514
Place of Detention	0.054	0.000
Race	0.047	0.241
Other Characteristic of Acc	0.045	0.265
No Other Characteristics	0.061	0.004
Held Incommunicado	0.043	0.471
No Incommunicado	0.059	0.004
Has Experience With Law	0.053	0.035
No Experience With Law	0.047	0.758
Is a Youth	0.050	0.096
Not a Youth	0.061	0.000
Deprivation of Needs	0.047	0.460
No Deprivation of Needs	0.063	0.005
Ideology of CA Panel	0.014	0.133
High Court Ideology	0.036	0.090
Lower Court Disposition	0.029	0.302
Habeas Corpus Claim	0.052	0.054
Heard En Banc	0.049	0.292

Probability Confession Overturned All at Mean = 0.052

Table 4.5: Testing For Differences Among the Circuits – D.C. As Baseline[75]

Independent Variable	Coefficient (r.s.e.)	Sig Level
First	2.46 (.71)	0.001
Second	-1.94 (.55)	0.000
Third	-1.54 (.63)	0.014
Fourth	-2.04 (.67)	0.002
Fifth	-1.50 (.46)	0.001
Sixth	-2.56 (.60)	0.000
Seventh	-1.25 (.50)	0.012
Eighth	-2.13 (.54)	0.000
Ninth	-1.06 (.47)	0.026
Tenth	-4.32 (.76)	0.000
Eleventh	-2.90 (.58)	0.000

Table 4.6: Testing For Differences Among the Circuits – Tenth Circuit as Baseline[76]

Independent Variable	Coefficient (r.s.e.)	Sig Level
First	2.46 (.71)	0.001
Second	2.38 (.71)	0.001
Third	2.78 (.79)	0.000
Fourth	2.28 (.86)	0.008
Fifth	2.82 (.68)	0.000
Sixth	1.76 (.75)	0.020
Seventh	3.08 (.74)	0.000
Eighth	2.19 (.72)	0.002
Ninth	3.26 (.73)	0.000
Eleventh	1.42 (.69)	0.040
D.C.	4.33 (.76)	0.000

Table 4.7: Frequencies of Circuit Exclusion of Confession

Circuit	# Decisions	# Exclusions	Percent
First	10	4	40
Second	50	12	24
Third	24	5	21
Fourth	37	13	35
Fifth	73	12	16
Sixth	30	5	17
Seventh	30	6	20
Eighth	52	10	19
Ninth	80	15	19
Tenth	48	2	4
Eleventh	60	13	22
D.C.	69	31	45
All Circuits	563	128	23
Supreme Court	57	39	68

Table 4.8: Mean Ideology of Circuit Panels

Circuit	Mean Ideology Score
First	0.73
Second	0.34
Third	0.48
Fourth	0.55
Fifth	0.61
Sixth	0.56
Seventh	0.42
Eighth	0.50
Ninth	0.42
Tenth	0.61
Eleventh	0.61
D.C.	0.66
All Circuits	0.53

CHAPTER 5

When the Supreme Court Speaks: An Analysis of Lower Court Treatment of Supreme Court Decisions

We have found that the Courts of Appeals need not worry much about the Supreme Court due to its lack of monitoring, but that they in fact do pay heed to the High Court in their decision making. Indeed, in confession cases, the Courts of Appeals take into account both Supreme Court precedent and the probability of reversal. Of course, the Courts of Appeals also pay heed to their own ideological preferences. But might we still be missing something?

As discussed earlier, lower courts needn't completely thwart the policy prescriptions of their principal in order to enact their preferences. Perhaps they decide cases creatively in order to both avoid unliked Supreme Court precedent and Supreme Court review. In this chapter, I look for such behavior qualitatively by tracing lower court treatment of two of the Supreme Court's decisions on confession, *Townsend v. Sain* (372 U.S. 293 (1963)) and *Bruton v. United States* (391 U.S. 123 (1968)). I adopt this approach because it is possible that the multivariate analysis finds compliance with the letter of the Supreme Court precedents, but not with their spirit. In other words, the lower court might know exactly which facts to mention and which to avoid in order to seem compliant. Only by reading the Courts of Appeals' treatment of Supreme Court precedent can we determine whether or not this is the case.

I choose these two particular cases for several reasons. First, neither was particularly salient. Some argue that less salient cases may be less complied with (see, e.g., Songer and Sheehan 1990). At the very least, it is worth testing. Second, they differ from one another in that the precedent established in *Townsend* was significantly related to

Courts of Appeals decisions (as seen in the last chapter), while that established in *Bruton* was not. By taking a closer look at the actual treatment of these precedents by the Courts of Appeals we may be able to uncover what is different or similar between these cases and suggest why, in the previous analysis, the Court's decision in *Bruton* did not exert a statistically significant influence on Courts of Appeals decision making. We can also uncover any covert noncompliance that may be taking place through this exercise.

In order to conduct this analysis, I "Shepardize" both *Townsend* and *Bruton,* reading each confession case that treats these two Supreme Court cases to determine whether the lower court is indeed paying heed to the Supreme Court prescription, or whether, through distinguishing the Supreme Court precedent from the case being decided, the Courts of Appeals avoid application of a distasteful precedent.

5.1 Vertical *Stare Decisis*

It is understandable that judges themselves disagree over the deference owed higher court rulings. One judge, openly hostile to the suggestion that he follow whatever the Supreme Court decides, said:

> …it cannot rationally be said that the state courts of all the states must necessarily follow every twist and turn of federal decisional law as it has developed in the many cases setting forth divergent views (Manwaring 1972:8).

Other judges join in the spirit of this judge's open defiance, making such statements as "[w]e follow them when we can't get around them" (Baum 1978:212); "[w]e cannot assume that the Supreme Court intended to deprive the highest court of an independent sovereign state of one of its traditional powers... the right to exercise a sound judicial discretion" (Murphy 1959:1021); or "[t]his Court's independent review of the relevant historical documents…convinces it that the United States Supreme Court has erred in its reading of history" (Caminker 1994:819).

More common, however, are statements from jurists sharing the spirit of this Wisconsin judge: "We are bound by the results and interpretations...in these high court decisions. Ours is not to reason why; ours but to review and apply" (*State v. Nusbaum,* 198 N.W.2d 650 at 653 (1972)). And that of a Florida justice who said "[w]e deem it to be our inescapable duty to abide by this decision of the United States Supreme Court [*Brown*[77]] interpreting the federal constitution" (Murphy 1959:1020). Learned Hand offered a similar sentiment: "I have always felt that it was the duty of an inferior court to suppress its own opinions and...try to prophesy what the appellate courts would do" (Baum 1978:212). Other federal judges agree: "The law as enumerated by the Supreme Court of the United States must be obeyed by all of us. If we do otherwise we will destroy our present form of Constitutional government" (*Evans v. Buchanan,* 256 F.2d 688 at 695).

Reputedly, lower court judges try to interpret the Supreme Court's will as closely as possible, leaving open the possibility that they sometimes err: "If the view we have expressed is incorrect there will be opportunity for its correction when the Supreme Court has spoken" (*Federated Mutual Implement and Hardware Insurance Co. v. Fairfax Equipment Company, Inc.,* 261 F.2d 207 at 207). They may also feign an inability to comprehend the current doctrine: "Federal laws? Nobody understands federal laws" (Johnson and Canon 1984:45; see also Murphy 1959). Further, some judges even attempt to anticipate what the Court will decide in the future in order to comply with it prospectively (Wasby 1972, Gruhl 1980). Clement Haynsworth, Nixon's original choice to fill the Fortas vacancy, illustrates this position in the language cited by the High Court in its overruling of *McNally v. Hill*, 293 U.S. 131 (1934): "Chief Judge Haynsworth reasoned that this Court would no longer follow *McNally*, which in his view represented a 'doctrinaire approach' based on an 'old jurisprudential concept' which has been 'thoroughly rejected by the Supreme Court in recent cases.'" (*Peyton v. Rowe*, 391 U.S. 54 (1968) at 57). They agreed with him. As Caminker eventually concludes, hierarchical adherence to precedent comports with the Constitution, and is probably necessary to a well-functioning judiciary.[78] Most studies conclude similarly, as discussed in Chapter 2; that the lower courts do indeed comply with Supreme Court decisions for the most part (Sanders 1995; Songer and Sheehan 1990; Johnson 1987; Songer 1987b;

Stidham and Carp 1982[79]; Gruhl 1980; Baum 1978; Murphy 1959). Not many take the "make my day" argument espoused by Amar (1994).[80]

However, compliance does, in fact, leave room for substantial influence, and permissive Supreme Court policies may well encourage innovation (Glick 1994). As one scholar put it, "There are many contexts in which the latitude of those charged with carrying out a policy is so substantial that studies of policy implementation should be turned on their heads. In these cases, policy is effectively 'made' by the people who implement it" (Johnson and Canon 1984:3).

My analysis will examine carefully whether the Courts of Appeals innovate, comply, or disregard the Supreme Court's mandate in the confession cases, at least with reference to two of them – one establishing the inadmissibility of codefendant's confessions and the other requiring plenary hearings in habeas corpus.

5.2 Compliance and Impact in Judicial Scholarship

The literature on judicial impact and compliance is voluminous, albeit somewhat contradictory. Canon contends that "[t]he impact literature is replete with hypotheses stemming from common sense suggestions, case studies or limited comparisons" (1973:130). Much proliferation has occurred since his writing which has confounded findings even more. Because decision making in the Courts of Appeals is particularly complicated (Songer and Haire 1992), many variables plausibly exert an influence upon a lower court's decision to dispose of a case in a certain manner. In most cases, the lower court has Supreme Court precedent to apply and interpret; its own policy preferences to pursue; and the relevant law, case facts, litigants, and arguments with which to contend.

The model offered in the last chapter attempted to measure Supreme Court impact by determining the extent to which variables identified as necessarily mattering to the determination of confession voluntariness by the Supreme Court actually matter to the Courts of Appeals. There, we found that the Courts of Appeals do indeed heed the High Court, as several precedential facts were considered by the Court of Appeals in its confession-case decision making.

However, as mentioned in Chapter 2, a lower court can be noncompliant without being openly so. By examining treatment of a couple of Supreme Court cases very closely, we are able to capture this differential compliance and determine whether the lower courts try in any way to avoid or limit the application of Supreme Court precedent. In addition, we can determine whether those lower courts that treat a precedent that comes out as statistically insignificant (according to Chapter 4) nonetheless comply with the precedent. In effect, I here test for the nuances missed in the multivariate analysis. This adds a depth of analysis that compliance and impact research often overlooks. In addition, it allows for further discussion of differences among the circuits. And it does so using non-salient cases, which is clearly the exception in impact and compliance work. In short, this sort of exploration may identify relationships worthy of future study and consideration.

5.3 Supreme Court Cases Under Analysis

As mentioned earlier, I have chosen the two precedents under consideration for two reasons. First, neither is a salient Supreme Court decision. Much impact analysis has been directed solely at salient or landmark cases, even though we may expect lower courts to adhere to a highly visible case like *Miranda*. Indeed, much research has been done on that decision, all of which concludes that the Courts of Appeals exhibit a high level of compliance with the Court's *Miranda* prescriptions (Beatty 1972; Canon 1973; Wasby 1973; Romans 1974; Songer and Sheehan 1990). By selecting non-salient cases for analysis, I study an environment in which the Courts of Appeals may feel freer to disregard the High Court's rulings.

The second reason for my choice of Supreme Court cases is that one was determined to be significant in the analysis in Chapter 4 and one was not. This allows for potential explanation of the differential treatment by the Courts of Appeals. Each of these cases, while not "salient" by Court scholars' standards, involves a formal alteration of precedent in an area in which strong views prevail. They involve criminal procedure and the rights afforded to those who would appeal their convictions. Surely judges have attitudes on such a matter, and liberal and conservatives most assuredly differ, if indeed attitudes influence the decision making of Courts of Appeals judges. Further, as we shall see in the next section, both Supreme Court decisions provide the Courts of Appeals with "wriggle room." Neither is a model of clarity. Reviewing courts, therefore, should be able to find reasons for affirming the petitioners' convictions, should they so desire.

This qualitative analysis proceeds as follows. First, a complete and detailed exposition of the two Supreme Court precedents under study is provided. Next, I discuss how Courts of Appeals cases treating these two precedents were identified. Finally, circuit by circuit and case by case, Courts of Appeals treatment of these Supreme Court precedents is examined. Conclusions about the connection between this analysis and the multivariate analysis presented in Chapter 4 are drawn at the end of the chapter.

5.3.1 *Townsend v. Sain,* 372 U.S. 293 (1963)

Townsend was convicted of murder and sentenced to death. After exhausting state remedies, he sought a writ of habeas corpus, claiming that his conviction violated the Fourteenth Amendment as his confession, obtained while under the influence of drugs – including what some view as a truth serum – was admitted over his objection. The District Court denied his application for habeas corpus without a hearing, and the Court of Appeals affirmed that denial. The Supreme Court reversed, deciding that the lower courts erred in denying the writ without a plenary evidentiary hearing.

In its opinion, the Court presents several conditions under which an accused, on habeas corpus, must receive a plenary hearing before the district court. First, "…where an applicant for a writ of habeas corpus alleges facts which, if proved, would entitle him to relief, the federal court to which the application is made has the power to receive evidence and try the facts anew" (at 312). Considerations which in certain cases may make exercise of that power mandatory are these: "where the facts are in dispute, the federal court in habeas corpus must hold an evidentiary hearing if the habeas applicant did not receive a full and fair evidentiary hearing in a state court, either at the time of the trial or in a collateral proceeding. In other words, a federal evidentiary hearing is required unless the state-court trier of fact has, after a full hearing, reliably found the relevant facts" (at 312-313). The Court further particularizes the controlling criteria. "We hold that a federal court must grant an evidentiary hearing to a habeas applicant under the following circumstances: If (1) the merits of the factual dispute were not resolved in the state hearing; (2) the state factual determination is not fairly supported by the record as a whole; (3) the fact-finding procedure employed by the state court was not adequate to afford a full and fair hearing; (4) there is a substantial allegation of newly discovered evidence; (5) the material facts were not adequately developed at the state-court hearing; or (6) for any reason it appears that the state trier of fact did not afford the habeas applicant a full and fair fact hearing" (at 313-314). A hearing may be avoided if the allegation of newly discovered evidence is "frivolous or incredible" (at 317), or if the evidence not developed was due to "the inexcusable neglect of the petitioner" (at 317).

Given this set of rules, I coded each confession case in the Court of Appeals which treated *Townsend* as either followed or not followed. Those that follow will either grant an evidentiary hearing, or provide one of the Supreme Court's reasons for not doing so (either the claim is frivolous, or the lack of evidence is due to petitioner culpability). Those coded as not following either simply refuse to grant an evidentiary hearing, or invalidly distinguish their case from *Townsend*.

Of course, we must take into account any subsequent treatment of the High Court itself in determining compliance. If the Supreme Court backs away from or extends its holding, surely that affects the lower courts' decisional process (Benesh and Reddick 2002). According to *Shepard's Citations*, the Court treated *Townsend* in two subsequent cases. In *Colorado v. Connelly,* 479 U.S. 157 (1986), the Court distinguished the facts in *Townsend* in order to rule on the voluntariness of a confession. Here, the Court is dealing with *Townsend* as a confession case rather than as a specification of when a plenary hearing in a habeas corpus case should occur, and so we would not expect *Connelly* to affect the Courts of Appeals' treatment of *Townsend*.[81]

The Court's second subsequent treatment of *Townsend* more substantially relates to our current concerns. In *Keeney v. Tamayo-Reyes,* 504 U.S. 1 (1992), the Court overruled a portion of the *Townsend* precedent. Respondent, a Cuban immigrant with almost no knowledge of English, collaterally attacked the plea he made in a state proceeding, arguing that his interpreter did not adequately interpret the *mens rea* element of manslaughter. Because of this, he contended that he did not know he was pleading no contest, but rather thought he agreed to be tried for manslaughter. The state court of appeals affirmed, and the state supreme court denied review.

Respondent then sought a writ of habeas corpus from the District Court, contending that material facts were not adequately developed, implicating the fifth circumstance of *Townsend*, and thereby entitling him to a federal evidentiary hearing on the constitutionality of his *nolo contendre* plea. The District Court ruled the situation a matter of petitioner neglect and denied the petition. The Court of Appeals reversed, ruling that *Townsend* and *Fay v. Noia,* 372 U.S. 391, required an evidentiary hearing "unless respondent had deliberately bypassed the orderly procedure of the state courts" (at 4).

The Supreme Court overruled those portions of *Townsend* and *Fay* that prescribed the "deliberate bypass standard [as] the correct standard for excusing a habeas petitioner's failure to develop a material fact in state-court proceedings" (at 5). Instead, the Court required use of the "cause-and-prejudice" standard: "As in cases of state procedural default, application of the cause-and-prejudice standard to excuse a state prisoner's failure to develop material facts in state court will appropriately accommodate concerns of finality, comity, judicial economy, and channeling the resolution of claims into the most appropriate form" (at 8). Thus, I expect that the Courts of Appeals will behave differently after the Supreme Court announced this change in precedent.

5.3.2 *Bruton v. United States,* 391 U.S. 123 (1968)

In this case, the joint trial of Bruton and one Evans resulted in their convictions for armed postal robbery. Evans did not take the stand, but a postal inspector testified as to his confession, in which Evans implicated Bruton. The trial judge instructed the jury that the confession could be used only against Evans, as per the Supreme Court's decision in *Delli Paoli v. United States*, 352 U.S. 232. Both appealed the decision and, on appeal, the Court of Appeals set aside Evans' conviction on the basis that the confession should not have been used against him. It affirmed Bruton's conviction, however. The Supreme Court, overruling *Delli Paoli*, held that the admission of Evans' confession without his testifying robbed Bruton of the opportunity to cross-examine him, thereby violating the Confrontation Clause of the Sixth Amendment. "Plainly, the introduction of Evans' confession added substantial, perhaps even critical, weight to the Government's case in a form not subject to cross-examination, since Evans did not take the stand. Petitioner thus was denied his constitutional right of confrontation" (at 127-128). "*Delli Paoli* assumed that this encroachment on the right to confrontation could be avoided by the instruction to the jury to disregard the inadmissible hearsay evidence. But, as we have said, that assumption has since been effectively repudiated...We...held [in *Jackson v. Denno,* 378 U.S. 368 (1964)] that a defendant is constitutionally entitled at least to have the trial judge first determine whether a confession was made voluntarily before submitting it to the jury for an assessment of its credibility. More specifically, we expressly rejected the proposition that a jury, when determining the confessor's guilt, could be relied on to ignore his confession of guilt should it find the confession involuntary" (at 128-129). "The fact of the matter is that too often such admonition against misuse is intrinsically ineffective in that the effect of such a nonadmissible declaration cannot be wiped from the brains of the jurors. The admonition therefore becomes a futile collection of words and fails of its purpose as a legal protection to defendants against whom such a declaration should not tell" (at 129 citing the dissent in *Delli Paoli*, Ibid at 247). "The naïve assumption that prejudicial effects can be overcome by instructions to the jury...all practicing lawyers know to be unmitigated fiction" (at 129, citing the concurrence in *Krulewitch v. U.S.* 336 U.S. 440 at 453).

Given the foregoing, the lower courts are compliant with *Bruton* only if they rule that the confession of a codefendant may not be introduced against the other even though the jury has been instructed not to consider it. However, as we shall see, there are several aspects of such confessions that the Court's decision does not cover; hence valid distinguishings arguably abound. In fact, the Court itself has distinguished *Bruton* several times, in effect, limiting its applicability.[82]

In *Frazier v. Cupp*, 394 U.S. 731 (1969), the Court found that an opening statement relating to a codefendant's confession did not violate the defendant's confrontation rights. The Court said that, in this case, because the prosecutor expected to produce the evidence as the codefendant was scheduled to testify, and because the prosecutor did not assert that the evidence was essential to his case, and because the court did give limiting instructions, no constitutional rights were infringed. "It may be that some remarks included in an opening or closing statement could be so prejudicial that a finding of error, or even constitutional error, would be unavoidable. But here we have no more than an objective summary of evidence which the prosecutor reasonably expected to produce…At least where the anticipated, and unproduced, evidence is not touted to the jury as a crucial part of the prosecution's case, it is hard for us to imagine that the minds of the jurors would be so influenced by such incidental statements during this long trial that they would not appraise the evidence objectively and dispassionately" (at 736, references omitted).

In *Dutton v. Evans*, 400 U.S. 74, (1970), the Court held that where a witness testifies, no confrontation question exists. "This case does not involve evidence in any sense "crucial" or "devastating," as did all the cases just discussed. It does not involve the use, or misuse, of a confession made in the coercive atmosphere of official interrogation, as did *Douglas*, *Brookhart*, *Bruton*, and *Roberts*…It does not involve a joint trial, as did *Bruton* and *Roberts*…The witness was vigorously and effectively cross-examined by defense counsel…His testimony, which was of peripheral significance at most, was admitted in evidence under a coconspirator exception to the hearsay rule long established under state statutory law…From the viewpoint of the Confrontation Clause, a witness under oath, subject to cross-examination, and whose demeanor can be observed by the trier of fact, is a reliable informant not only as to what he has seen but also as to what he has heard" (at 87).

In 1985, the Court said that the introduction of a codefendant's confession for the nonhearsay purpose of rebutting respondent's testimony that his confession was a coerced copy of his codefendant's was affirmed (*Tennessee v. Street*, 471 U.S. 409 (1985)). The State relied on a confession that respondent made to the Sheriff. Respondent asserted that his confession was coercively derived from his accomplice's written confession, as read to him by the Sheriff. In rebuttal, the State called the Sheriff, and in so doing, the Sheriff read the confession of the co-defendant to prove differences between the two statements. The Court held that "the *nonhearsay* aspect of the accomplice's confession – not to prove what happened at the murder scene but to prove what happened when respondent confessed – raises no Confrontation Clause concerns. The Clause's fundamental role in protecting the right of cross-examination was satisfied by the Sheriff's presence on the witness stand" (at 413-414). The trial judge did give instructions on the use of the accomplice's confession, and these were deemed adequate.

In 1987, the Court decided that it is acceptable to admit the confession of a codefendant so long as it is redacted as to the other defendant (*Richardson v. Marsh*, 481 U.S. 200, (1987)). In this case, a codefendant's confession was admitted only as to said codefendant, and all reference to petitioner was deleted. In fact, the confession was redacted such that it appeared that only the confessor and another person were involved in any criminal activity. Petitioner contends that, in addition to other admissible evidence, the jury could infer the presence of the petitioner in her codefendant's statement. Over a Brennan/Marshall dissent, the Court "hold[s] that the Confrontation Clause is not violated by the admission of a nontestifying codefendant's confession with a proper limiting instruction when, as here, the confession is redacted to eliminate not only the defendant's name, but any reference to his or her existence. We express no opinion on the admissibility of a confession in which the defendant's name has been replaced with a symbol or neutral pronoun" (at 211).

Incidentally, the Court decided that *Bruton* was to be applied retroactively (*Roberts v. Russell*, 392 U.S. 293 (1968)), and that errors under *Bruton* were subject to harmless error analysis (*Harrington v. California*, 395 U.S. 250 (1969)). The lower courts also cite other Supreme Court cases in support of their distinguishing a given case from the Supreme Court's policy prescription in *Bruton* (*Nelson v.*

O'Neil, 402 U.S. 622 (1971), *Cruz v. New York* 481 U.S. 186 (1987), *Parker v. Randolph*, 442 U.S. 62 (1979), and *California v. Green*, 399 U.S. 149 (1970)). These will be discussed as we review the treatment of *Bruton* by the various circuits. While these decisions may have affected the lower courts' treatment of *Bruton*, they did not formally treat *Bruton*, at least according to *Shepard's*.

5.4 Identification of Courts of Appeals Cases

Tarr (1977) offers useful definitions of compliance and noncompliance, which I employ in this study in order to identify relevant Courts of Appeals decisions for inclusion in my analysis. Compliance involves "...proper application of standards enunciated by the Supreme Court in deciding all cases raising similar or related questions" (1977:35), while noncompliance "...involves a failure to apply — or properly apply — those standards" (1977:35). Using these definitions, I selected cases via *Shepard's United States Supreme Court Citations*.[83]

Songer cautions against the use of *Shepard's* in impact case selection, for he says that "The impact of a given Supreme Court decision should be assessed by examining all decisions below in which the principles announced by the Court are relevant to the resolution of the issues presented to the lower court" (1987a:570). He cites the possibility that lower courts merely ignore Supreme Court precedent as a means of noncompliance. While I agree theoretically, several scholars have found evidence to mitigate the seriousness of this problem for studying the Courts of Appeals.

In order to determine whether lower courts were employing this strategy, Reddick and I (2002) analyzed Courts of Appeals treatment of Supreme Court alterations of precedent.[84] We argued that these cases, if treated by the lower courts, should surely be cited as the High Court had explicitly changed the precedent to be relied upon. If the lower court ignored these cases, the potential for the reality of Songer's caution would be quite large. In order to determine whether the Courts of Appeals ignored Supreme Court overrulings, we identified common West Key numbers between the overruled and overruling decisions, ascertaining the issues that were the basis of the overruling,[85] and obtained every lower court decision under those keys from the year of the overruling decision to 1999. This generated several thousand cases. We examined a sample of these lower court decisions to determine if in fact they ignored the change in precedent and thus were noncompliant — behavior which *Shepard's Citations* would fail to identify. We found not a single opinion that overtly ignored an overruling decision. On the basis of this search, we concluded that the Courts of Appeals do not simply disregard an objectionable precedent, but rather find more subtle ways to avoid it. These courts may well differ from the state supreme courts Songer used in his illustration. In either case, as many have found, they do not seem to openly avert Supreme Court precedent (Benesh and Reddick 2002; Songer 1987b; Songer and Sheehan 1990).

In addition, a recent study has found the coding done by *Shepard's* to be quite valid and reliable, especially for the very positive (followed) and very negative treatments (overruled, limited) (Spriggs and Hansford 2000). Although they find that those multifaceted or neutral treatments should probably be coded for their validity (distinguished, explained, harmonized) that they found the others to be both valid and reliable is a good indication that our fears in using *Shepard's* have been largely unfounded. Thus my use of *Shepard's Citations* is appropriate.[86]

I utilized *Shepard's* to identify the Courts of Appeals' treatment of Supreme Court decisions. In order to assess a circuit court's treatment of either *Bruton* or *Townsend* (either followed, limited, criticized, questioned, or distinguished), I carefully evaluated the courts' opinions. My inquiry did not address the propriety of whether the Court of Appeals should have provided the specified *Shepard's* treatment to either *Bruton* or *Townsend,* but rather, whether the *Shepard's* treatment accurately characterized the precedent in light of the facts of the Court of Appeals case.[87] I coded all of the circuit court cases as having either "followed" or "not followed" an overruling decision, or eliminated the citation from the analysis.[88]

5.5 Courts of Appeals' Compliance with *Bruton* and *Townsend*

I proceed on a circuit-by-circuit basis, beginning with *Bruton*. Tables 5.1 and 5.2 contain a summary of circuit treatment of the two precedents.

In the following two sections, I assess the way the individual circuits treated the Supreme Court's decisions in *Bruton* and *Townsend.* I will not discuss every case heard by each of the circuits; rather, I will briefly summarize the "valid" distinguishings made by each circuit; i.e., those I have coded as "followed, " and then discuss those cases which I have deemed to "not follow" the relevant Supreme Court decision. Patterns should be discovered within the circuits and conclusions duly drawn. Do note that I accept *Shepard's* decision when it codes a case as "following" for *Bruton*. Therefore, I do not discuss these cases.[89] For reasons given in the *Townsend* section, I read and code all of the cases treating that decision, however, including those designated as "following" by *Shepard's*.

Bruton v. United States

5.5.1 The First Circuit

The First Circuit treated *Bruton* in five confession cases. In four of those cases, *Shepard's* coded the circuit as having distinguished *Bruton*, and in one, it coded it as following the Supreme Court precedent. (Again, I accept *Shepard's* determination of followed and do not discuss said cases here.) I find the first few cases to dutifully follow *Bruton*, while the most recent seemingly avoids the Court's precedent. In the distinguishing cases that I have coded as following *Bruton*, the circuit differentiated between its decision and the Court's for the following reasons: lack of a jury (*U.S. v. Castro,* 413 F.2d. 891 (1969)); a codefendant who was indeed available for cross-examination (*LaFrance v. Bohlinger,* 499 F.2d. 29 (1974)); and the presence of a conspiracy, thereby invoking an exception to the hearsay rule (*Grieco v. Meachum,* 533 F.2d. 713 (1976)). All of these seem to comport with the spirit of the Supreme Court decision.

However, I judge the last of the First Circuit's cases not to follow *Bruton* (*U.S. v. Smith,* 46 F.3d. 1223 (1995)). In this case, a codefendant called an authority on professional responsibility to the stand. Before he did so, the court indicated that his testimony applied only to Cohen, one of the defendants. This authority testified that Cohen had come to him with a professional responsibility problem. "Documentation which he had prepared and which was complete and on file had been changed by three people [identified in the testimony as a former officer, a former director, and a manager of a bank] in their indication to him when they met with him" (at 1228). In other words, these three individuals told Cohen that they had changed the documents he had finished and filed, and Cohen went to this authority on professional responsibility to talk about it. Cohen's codefendants moved for a mistrial citing *Bruton*.

"The court submitted the case to the jury because the *Bruton* error (if any) occurred during the last day of testimony in a lengthy trial, and might be mooted by an acquittal. In addition, the harmfulness of the error would be more apparent in light of the verdicts" (at 1228-1229). All of the defendants were convicted and the district court found that there had been an error under *Bruton,* but that said error was harmless beyond a reasonable doubt. The first circuit agreed, saying that "Admittedly, Cohen's statement might tend to incriminate Smith and Devaney [the codefendants] by showing that the co-conspirators met to discuss damage control. In this sense, however, the statement falls far outside the pale of the 'powerfully incriminating' evidence that produces *Bruton* errors" (at 1229). The court concluded that it was "merely cumulative of the government's case" (at 1229).

Since the jury convicted even Cohen, it must not have believed him that the others admitted their conspiracy to him. Therefore, the district court was affirmed. While the Court has advocated the use of redacted confessions, it seems that in this case the jury could easily infer that the codefendants were those named by the Professor as identified by their occupations. Therefore, I consider this case not to have followed *Bruton*. Thus, in four of its five cases the First Circuit conformed to *Bruton*.

5.5.2 The Second Circuit

The Second Circuit treated *Bruton* 18 times, 12 of which *Shepard's* identified as distinguished and 6 of which were listed as following. I have coded all 18 as following *Bruton*, although I do discuss one that is on the edge of compliance.

In the followed cases that *Shepard's* notes as distinguishing, the lower court draws distinctions between its case and the Supreme Court's such as: though the complaining codefendant confessed, independent evidence of his guilt was overwhelming (*U.S. v. Wallack,* 414 F.2d. 246 (1969)); the error was harmless due to the wealth of evidence against the accused (*U.S. v. LaVallee,* 415 F.2d. 150 (1969)); the well-established co-conspirator hearsay exception (*U.S. v. Littman,* 421 F.2d. 981 (1970)); the confessing codefendant took the stand (*U.S. v. Mancusi,* 441 F.2d. 1073 (1971)); and the redacted statement in no way inculpated the co-defendants, in fact not referencing other persons at all (*U.S. v. Trudo,* 449 F.2d. 649 (1971).

I find *U.S. v. Follette,* 430 F.2d. 1055 (1970), to be a close call. Nelson (appellant) and Biggins were jointly tried and convicted of murder. Nelson claimed a *Bruton* violation because two confessions made by Biggins were introduced at the joint trial, and Biggins did not take the stand. Biggins' statement did not name Nelson as his colleague, but referred to a man known as "Oliver." Biggins, however, gave a physical description of Oliver that more or less fit Nelson's description. The circuit relied on the presence or absence of a goatee as evidence that Nelson was not "clearly inculpated by his general resemblance to 'Oliver' at the time of trial" (at 1057). The circuit reasoned that these statements "were not the type of 'powerfully incriminating' statements to which the Court had reference in *Bruton*" (at 1058). Biggins said that he had run into Oliver earlier in the evening and that they then proceeded to the Uptown Bar where the robbery and murder occurred.

If the jury believed that Nelson was Oliver, surely this is incriminating evidence. Nonetheless, the circuit said it was not a vital part of the government's case, and that there was other evidence linking Nelson to the crime, including the identification of eyewitnesses. In addition, Biggins' statement that Oliver was the principal actor in the murder was directly contradicted by the eyewitnesses, who all agreed that Biggins was the primary robber and did the actual killing. The judge did "carefully instruct…the jury that these statements could be considered only with respect to the defendant Biggins and that they were not to be considered in any way with respect to the innocence or guilt of the defendant Nelson" (at 1059). "We find the possibility that the jury made an inference from [the] testimony that it would not have made in any event, and that this inference made the difference between acquittal and conviction for [appellant], far too remote to meet the *Bruton* tests" (at 1059, citations deleted). While I code this decision as following, some may disagree.

Because the circuit generally made valid distinctions, and in some cases even made stronger prescriptions than the Supreme Court (*U.S. v. Danzey,* 594 F.2d. 905 (1979)), I consider the Second Circuit compliant with *Bruton.*

5.5.3 The Fourth Circuit[90]

The Fourth Circuit treated *Bruton* in 7 confession cases, four of which distinguished and three of which followed, according to *Shepard's*. I judge them all compatible with *Bruton*. The circuit distinguished for various reasons: (1) There was an adequate redaction and so the confession does not refer specifically to the codefendants (*Close v. U.S.,* 450 F.2d. 152 (1971), and *U.S. v. Grant,* 549 F.2d. 942 (1977)); (2) the admission of the fact that the codefendant remained silent in the face of accusations by his accomplice was harmless due to the overwhelming evidence of guilt (*Miller v. Cox,* 457 F.2d. 700 (1972), and *Folston v. Allsbrook,* 691 F.2d. 184 (1982)); (3) the confessions were interlocking, as discussed by a plurality of the Supreme Court in *Parker v. Randolph*, 442 U.S. 62 (1979) (*U.S. v. Smith,* 792 F.2d. 441 (1986)); and (4) the testimony was not incriminating against the codefendant (*U.S. v. Crockett,* 813 F.2d. 1310 (1987)).

In *U.S. v. Truslow,* 530 F.2d. 257 (1975), the Fourth Circuit scrupulously guarded the codefendant's right to confront witnesses against him or her. While they did not find *Bruton* violations in all of the statements admitted at trial, they deemed the cumulative effect of all of the admissions to be such that the defendants were deprived of their constitutional right to confrontation. They deem the failure of the trial court to order severance or take other preventive action to be enough to reverse its judgment. The Fourth Circuit correctly distinguished its cases from *Bruton*, and in some cases, went even further than the Supreme Court in protecting an accused's confrontation rights.

5.5.4 The Fifth Circuit

The Fifth Circuit treated *Bruton* in more confession cases than any of the others – 37. *Shepard's* coded 26 as distinguishing *Bruton* and 11 as following it. I have coded two of the Circuit's decisions as failing to follow *Bruton*, in that they avoided the application of the *Bruton* precedent.

Valid distinctions made by this Circuit include the following: the statement did not refer to the codefendant (*White v. U.S.,* 415 F.2d. 292 (1969)); the codefendants all testified (*Roberts v. U.S.,* 416 F.2d. 1216 (1969)); the government did not place the statements into evidence, nor did they incriminate appellant (*U.S. v. Venere,* 416 F.2d. 144 (1969)); the statement did not incriminate the defendant (*U.S. v. Gibson,* 416 F.2d. 326 (1969), *U.S. v. Pollard,* 509 F.2d. 601 (1975), *U.S. v. Grillo,* 527 F.2d. 1344 (1979), and *U.S. v. Castro,* 596 F.2d. 674 (1979)); the codefendant was available for and was cross-examined (*U.S. v. Johnson,* 478 F.2d. 1129 (1973), and *U.S. v. Maddox,* 492 F.2d. 104 (1974); the court both redacted the confessions and excluded the statements at issue so that they were not mentioned before the jury (*U.S. v. Wilson,* 500 F.2d. 715 (1974)); the codefendant made the statement while in the course of a conspiracy (*U.S. v. Burroughs,* 650 F.2d. 595 (1981)); the statements do not reflect guilt on the codefendant (*U.S. v. Coppola,* 788 F.2d. 303 (1986))

The first of this Circuit's noncompliant decisions was *Migliore v. U.S.,* 409 F.2d. 786 (1969). Because the evidence presented from a statement by Migliore about Mingo (the two codefendants in the case) was made during the commission of a crime, they were admissible. This conforms to *Bruton*. However, a statement made by Mingo about Migliore was admitted because "Migliore made no objection at the trial to the admission of this testimony" (at 788). This arguably violates the spirit of *Bruton*.

The second questionable decision was one that the circuit heard en banc with a lengthy opinion (*Hoover v. Beto,* 467 F.2d. 516 (1972)). At issue was a Texas law that "permits inculpatory references against an accomplice to be heard by the jury, subject to limiting instructions by the court to regard the whole confession as evidence only against the declarant confessor" (at 529). This seems to directly violate the Court's holding in *Bruton*. However, the Circuit does have a plausible reason for excepting this case from *Bruton's* holding: the trial was not joint, but rather that of an accomplice, which was severed from the trial of the principals. Because the state makes the guilt of the principals prerequisite to the conviction of an accomplice, the Circuit argued that the admission of the confession was justified and did not violate the accomplice's confrontation rights. Further, the majority pointed to the examination of the prospective jurors as to their ability to consider a confession in this way saying the court was protective of the accused's rights. Therefore, it did not consider the trial court's conclusion that a limiting instruction could protect the accomplice erroneous.

The dissenters, however, asserted that references to the accomplice could surely have been taken out of the confession and the prosecution could have still proved the guilt of the principals while protecting the confrontation rights of the defendant. It is my determination that the Supreme Court may well agree with the dissenters and so I coded this decision as not following *Bruton*. The Court went to great lengths in *Bruton* to discuss the meaninglessness of limiting instructions, and this Circuit relied upon the curative effect of them in admitting the statements. This is incompatible with the Court's decision. I think this Circuit, while evidencing some division *en banc*, is apt to accept reasoning which, in effect, thwarts Supreme Court precedent, though even it most often follows the Supreme Court precedent on point.

5.5.5 The Sixth Circuit

The Sixth Circuit treated *Bruton* in 18 confession cases, distinguishing 8 cases, following in 9, and limiting it once. I consider all 18 cases compliant with *Bruton*, although two arguably are not. The Circuit, however, does assert that it "has sought faithfully to follow the teachings of *Bruton*..." (*Randolph v. Parker,* 575 F.2d 1178 at 1182). It seemingly does not overstate its aims or behavior.

Valid distinguishings include the following: the confessing codefendant took the stand (although he did deny making the statement) (*U.S. v. Sims,* 430 F.2d. 1089 (1970)); the appellant himself confessed, and the codefendant making incriminating statements also took the stand – there was also much evidence against him apart from the confessions (*Farmer v. Kropp,* 445 F.2d. 5 (1971)); codefendant was a co-conspirator and the statement was made in furtherance of the conspiracy (*U.S. v. McManus,* 560 F.2d. 747 (1977), and *U.S. v. Kendricks,* 623 F.2d. 1165 (1980)); and the trial was before a judge not a jury (*Rogers v. McMackin,* 884 F.2d. 252 (1989)).

The two questionable cases are *Yates v. U.S.,* 418 F.2d. 1228 (1969), and *Childs v. Cardwell,* 452 F.2d. 541 (1971). In the first, the Court made a redaction that I am not certain would pass scrutiny had the Supreme Court reviewed the case. The trial court had "masked" the written confession so that the other codefendants' names could not be read by the jury. The clerk then photographed the confession and entered it as evidence. One of the codefendants claimed that his identity was not sufficiently concealed.

In the second problematic case, the Circuit did not find for the appellant because he did not object to the admission of the testimony of a police officer as to the statements of a codefendant. The Court argued that, because the codefendant can cross-examine the officer, and, additionally, since the codefendant was already convicted, the codefendant could have been called as a hostile witness, the appellant's confrontation rights were not violated. The Circuit found the error harmless. Nonetheless, the Circuit arguably did adhere to the *Bruton* holding, and so I find very little evidence of any noncompliance.

5.5.6 The Seventh Circuit

The Seventh Circuit treated *Bruton* in 20 confession cases, 15 of which *Shepard's* labeled "distinguished" and 5 of which it labeled "followed." I deem all of these cases compliant with *Bruton*. Examples of this Circuit's valid distinguishings include: the statements were not incriminating and, further, the confessing codefendant was a witness at the trial and thereby subject to cross-examination (*U.S. v. Hoffa,* 402 F.2d. 380 (1968)); the appellant did not move for a severance, an additional codefendant testified (and was cross-examined) to the same things in the admitted statement, the statement was redacted, and the defendant himself confessed (*U.S. v. Pate,* 418 F.2d. 1028 (1970)); the agent did not identify a codefendant as his source of the information until the appellant cross-examined him, hence there was no reversible error (454 F.2d. 1208 (1972)); the defendant himself confessed, substantially in the same words as his codefendant (*U.S. v. Spinks,* 470 F.2d. 64 (1972)); the co-conspirator exception to the hearsay rule occurred (*U.S. v. Donner et al.,* 497 F.2d. 184 (1974)); and the statement was redacted and the jury warned twice to use it only against the confessing codefendant (*U.S. v. Kreiser,* 15 F.3d. 635 (1994)). This Circuit clearly complied with *Bruton*.

5.5.7 The Eighth Circuit

The Eighth Circuit treated *Bruton* in 12 cases, 6 of which *Shepard's* classified as distinguished, 5 followed, and 1 limited. One decision is a bit questionable, but the others all validly distinguish themselves from *Bruton.* Some reasons for the distinctions are the following: both defendants confessed, and the codefendant in question took the stand (*U.S. v. Fountain,* 449 F.2d. 629 (1971)); the codefendant took the stand and denied making the statement (*U.S. v. Valenzuela,* 521 F.2d. 414 (1975)); and the co-conspirator exception to the hearsay rule (*U.S. v. Kelley et al.,* 526 F.2d. 615 (1975)).

The one case that gives pause is *Tasby v. U.S.,* 451 F.2d. 394 (1971). The Circuit deemed harmless the introduction of in-custody confessions made by each of the defendants. The testifying witnesses avoided any specific reference of one codefendant to the others, except that reference was made to the fact that one of the accomplices had a noticeable eye defect. Only the appellant had such a defect and so was easily identifiable. However, the court concluded this to be harmless error because law enforcement officers had arrested him during his actual participation in the crime. It seems that the Circuit could have remanded the case back to try the appellant without the indirect identification, but chose not to. While I see this as following *Bruton* for the most part, the opposite argument could also be made.

Overall then, the Eighth Circuit, like the others, implemented the *Bruton* decision.

5.5.8 The Ninth Circuit

The Ninth Circuit treated *Bruton* in 15 cases, ten of which distinguished it and five of which followed it. I have determined that all but one of this court's decisions adhered to *Bruton,* while two are seemingly indeterminable. Those that distinguish it do so validly for reasons that include the following: the codefendants took the stand (*Santoro v. U.S.,* 402 F.2d. 920 (1968), and *Rios-Ramirez v. U.S.,* 403 F.2d. 1016)); the appellant was tried by the court not by a jury (*Cockrell v. Oberhauser,* 413 F.2d. 256 (1969)); the codefendant's statement was used only in the opening statement (*U.S. v. Maurice,* 416 F.2d. 234 (1969)); the statement only mentioned "other participants" (*U.S. v. Akers et al.,* 542 F.2d. 770 (1976)); admission was harmless error because appellant made the same statement rendering the codefendant's statement merely corroborative (*U.S. v. Espericueta-Reyes,* 631 F.2d. 616 (1980)); the challenged statements were made by the defendant himself (*U.S. v. Gonzales,* 749 F.2d. 1329 (1984)); and the statement was not hearsay (*White v. Lewis et al.,* 874 F.2d. 599 (1989)).

In *U.S. v. Barragan,* 453 F.2d. 386 (1971), the Circuit Court completely denies and does not discuss the alleged *Bruton* violation because "no proper objection was made to lay the basis for the application of *Bruton*. We think the statements of the two (husband and wife) were admissible on the government's case in chief" (at 387). Completely rejecting the claim of a husband and wife that one statement implicated the other is questionable indeed. I deem this case evidence of the Ninth Circuit's imperfect compliance.

The other two cases with which I take issue are *U.S. v. Vissars,* 596 F.2d. 400 (1979), and *U.S. v. Arambula-Ruiz,* 987 F.2d. 599 (1993). In the first, I question the court's holding because the dissent disagrees with a factual statement of the majority. Here, the majority finds that if there were error in the admission of the codefendant's statement it was harmless, due to the court's belief that the "evidence of guilt is...overwhelming" (at 404). The dissenter disagrees, saying "I do not believe that the *Bruton* error was harmless beyond a reasonable doubt. The case against Keenberg was strong, but I do not believe that it was overwhelming" (at 404). Because there is no way to determine the accuracy of the majority's argument, I deem the Circuit to have followed here, noting my reservations.

The other debatable case deals with the incriminating nature of the statements admitted at trial. The statement was redacted, but both parties agreed that it was inadmissible. "However, they dispute its prejudicial effect" (at 605). "We have found no cases which address the precise issue presented here: whether an incriminating question posed by defense counsel and based upon a defendant's confession creates reversible *Bruton* error" (at 605). The Circuit did indeed confront a matter not directly addressed by *Bruton*. It decided that no error occurred because the question was stricken before it was answered and was followed immediately by a limiting instruction from the judge. This may well be true, but it is a case that could have plausibly gone either way. Merely asking a question may influence a jury's decision. Here, the Circuit gives the jury the benefit of the doubt; a benefit I am not altogether convinced would also be given the jury by the High Court. All in all, however, the Ninth Circuit, like the others, is largely compliant with the Supreme Court.

5.5.9 The Tenth Circuit

The Tenth Circuit treated *Bruton* in 11 confession cases, ten of which distinguished it, and one that followed it. I consider all to have followed the High Court prescription, although one case may be deemed questionable. Reasons for the Tenth Circuit to distinguish *Bruton* mostly fall into one of two categories: the codefendant testified (*Thomas v. U.S.,* 409 F.2d. 730 (1969), *McHenry v. U.S.,* 420 F.2d. 927 (1970), *Duggar v. U.S.,* 434 F.2d. 345 (1970), *U.S. v. Gurule,* 437 F.2d. 239 (1970), *U.S. v. Steel,* 458 F.2d. 1164 (1972), and *U.S. v. Troutman,* 458 F.2d. 217 (1972)); or the conspiracy exception to the hearsay rule applied (*U.S. v. Cox,* 449 F.2d. 679 (1971), *U.S. v. Montgomery,* 582 F.2d. 514 (1978), and *U.S. v. Rogers et al.,* 652 F.2d. 972 (1981)).

The one questionable case is *U.S. v. Jackson et al.,* 482 F.2d. 1167 (1973). The circuit panel found that the admission of several exhibits did not violate petitioner's *Bruton* protections. The appellant argued that the admission of the exhibits improperly stigmatized him without the opportunity for cross-examination. The court found that the exhibits implicated only the one defendant and did not harm the appellant. It said that the exhibits "can in no way be considered so powerfully incriminating to Jackson that limiting instructions would not sufficiently protect his rights" (at 1175). The panel, therefore, found that the limiting instructions were adequately protective of appellant's constitutional rights. This holding, while seemingly consistent with *Bruton*, is arguable. In all, however, the Tenth Circuit was quite cognizant of the Court's holding in *Bruton* and complied with it.

5.5.10 The Eleventh Circuit

The Eleventh Circuit treated *Bruton* in 10 confession cases. In five, *Shepard's* deemed the Circuit to have distinguished its case from *Bruton* and in the other half it asserted that *Bruton* was followed. I find that the Circuit followed *Bruton* in all but one case, and that another is questionable. In distinguishing *Bruton*, the Circuit noted the following: the codefendant merely agreed with the appellant's version of the facts (*Westbrook v. Zant,* 704 F.2d. 1487 (1983)); the statement was not directly incriminating and it was made in the prosecution's opening statement which is not admitted as evidence (*U.S. v. Jimenez,* 780 F.2d. 975 (1986)); and that the statement was admitted only toward the voluntariness of the confession and so was not hearsay (*Cargill v. Turpin,* 120 F.3d. 1366 (1997)).

One case does not seem to comply with *Bruton* (*Bowden v. Francis,* 733 F.2d. 740 (1984)). In this case, the panel decided that the admission of a codefendant's confession was harmless because the appellant "suggests nothing that he could have gained by cross-examining Hardaway on the subject" (at 757). Since the Supreme Court has found that all have a right to confront witnesses against them, this justification is seemingly inapposite to the Court's preferred policy. The Circuit claims that the evidence was overwhelming and that the appellant did make the jury aware of the inculpatory statement before the testimony in question. In addition, the prosecution did not mention the problem statement again in his closing.

While the Circuit seemed to avoid *Bruton* in this case, it did follow it in the others, except for one other potentially problematic case (*U.S.*

v. Arias, 984 F.2d. 1139 (1993)). Here, the Court relied upon a redaction that merely substituted the codefendant's names with "wife" or "husband." This redaction hardly seems to maintain the confrontation rights of the two codefendants. The Court maintained that the statements were not confessions, but rather "attempts by the parties to exculpate themselves" (at 1142) and therefore, were not essential to the prosecution of their cases. However, the use of confessions redacted only to replace a codefendant's name with "wife" or "husband" is highly suspect.

5.5.11 The D.C. Circuit

The District of Columbia Circuit treated *Bruton* in six confession cases. In half it followed *Bruton*, and in the other half, according to *Shepard's*, it distinguished it. I find that five of the decisions follow *Bruton* and one does not.

In two of the valid distinguishings, evidence was excluded as hearsay and the jury admonished not to consider it (*U.S. v. Burroughs,* 935 F.2d. 292 (1991)) and the confession was redacted and a neutral pronoun inserted (*U.S. v. Washington,* 952 F.2d. 1402 (1991)); therefore, no *Bruton* violation occurred. In the invalid distinguishing, the Court admitted the statements of a codefendant merely because they were "reliable." The panel says "Judd's statements to Young and Thomas were reliable. Judd's statements were not contained in a confession to law enforcement officials. He made the statements to lay persons with whom he had no motive or incentive to diminish his role by shifting blame; quite the contrary, Judd's statements revealed conduct beyond his mere presence in the area where Copeland was seen and shot" (at 741). The Court added that even if these statements were admitted in error, that error was harmless due to the overwhelming evidence against both defendants. It seems that a reliance on the reliability of the statements was not the aim of the High Court, and therefore, I think the D.C. Circuit strayed from the Supreme Court's policy prescription.

Townsend v. Sain

The Circuits' treatment of *Townsend* admits of a presentation different from that I accorded *Bruton*. In *Townsend*, the Supreme Court laid out a detailed set of six conditions (as mentioned in section 5.3.1), any one of which required a district court judge to provide an accused, on habeas corpus, with an evidentiary hearing. Reading cases that involve a confession provides a reasonably objective indication of circuit court compliance, or the lack thereof: i.e., the degree of detail the circuit panel's opinion provides in determining whether or not a *Townsend*-type evidentiary hearing is required. Although the High Court specified in detail the conditions that require a hearing, many of those details contain vague and undefined terms; e.g., "full and fair," "substantial allegation," "fairly supported," "adequately developed." Thus, I consider *Townsend* complied with if the circuit panel either returned the case to the federal district court to apply *Townsend* or to evaluate its applicability (most always the former) or, if in denying the habeas petitioner's plea, it carefully scrutinized lower court records and presented reasons – based on *Townsend* – why the lower court adhered to the High Court's strictures. Therefore, I read all treatments afforded to *Townsend* by the circuits, even if *Shepard's* noted that *Townsend* was followed. Following can be cosmetic here, so I investigate each treatment further.

5.5.12 The First Circuit

The First Circuit treated only one confession case with reference to *Townsend*. *Shepard's* coded that treatment as distinguishing *Townsend*, but upon reading the lower court seems to follow the Supreme Court's prescription. The court exhaustively recounted the facts in the case, finding that the influence of alcohol was not considered by the state court and so the defendant deserved a hearing on the matter. The First Circuit, then, in its single treatment afforded *Townsend* due deference.

5.5.13 The Second Circuit

The Second Circuit treated *Townsend* in three cases, all of which *Shepard's* coded as following the Supreme Court's treatment of the matter. All of them reverse the conviction, remanding the case to the lower court for evidentiary hearings. Hence, compliance.

5.5.14 The Third Circuit

The Third Circuit treated *Townsend* in four confession cases – again all of which are coded by *Shepard's* as having followed the Supreme Court precedent. In one case (*U.S. v. Rundle,* 389 F.2d. 47 (1968), one of the judges on the panel dissented. In another, (*U.S. v. Yeager,* 453 F.2d. 1001 (1971), a judge specially concurred reluctantly agreeing that the *Townsend* principle was applicable to the case at hand. Given the dissent and the special concurrence, one may conclude that the Third Circuit is somewhat less willing to comply with *Townsend* than was the Second Circuit, even though it reported no such non-compliant decisions.

5.5.15 The Fourth Circuit

The Fourth Circuit considered three confession cases, with all three following the precedent set in *Townsend.* In this Circuit, compliance occurred even though two of the cases affirmed lower court decisions. The case that was reversed and remanded construed *Townsend* in a manner definitely sympathetic to the petitioner (*Edwards v. Garrison,* 529 F.2d. 1374 (1975)).

5.5.16 The Fifth Circuit

The Fifth Circuit treated *Townsend* in ten confession cases, all of which *Shepard's* deemed to follow *Townsend.* However, in carefully reading even those that *Shepard's* coded as followed, there is evidence that this Circuit was reluctant to comply with the High Court's prescription. In the first of the confession cases, *Allison v. Holman,* 326 F.2d. 294 (1963), the panel treated *Townsend* in a rather offhand fashion, doing little more than simply saying – in a conclusory fashion, without elaboration or explanation – that the lower courts had complied with *Townsend.* I read this as an indication that the Circuit did in fact avoid application of the precedent, by merely affirming summarily the lower court. Perhaps this is a common tactic employed by the Courts of Appeals when it wishes to avoid application of a disapproved Supreme

Court precedent. Circuit panels behaved similarly in two other cases: *Gotcher v. Beto,* 444 F.2d. 696 (1971) and in *McMillin v. Beto,* 447 F.2d. 453 (1971).

While I've accepted the panel's decision in *Dempsey v. Wainwright,* 471 F.2d. 604 (1973), as followed, it nonetheless applied *Townsend* in a slipshod fashion. The judges did give reasons why the lower court complied with *Townsend*, but they did so in a hair splitting fashion, rather than one consistent with the spirit of *Townsend.*

In *Burns v. Beto,* 371 F.2d. 598 (1967), the panel did follow *Townsend*, however, granting the appellant an evidentiary hearing. But a district court judge on the panel dissented, rather clearly rejecting *Townsend*. Overall then, it is rather apparent that the Fifth Circuit only marginally complied with *Townsend*.

5.5.17 The Sixth Circuit

The Sixth Circuit treated *Townsend* in three confession cases, two of which *Shepard's* considers to have distinguished the High Court's decision, and one to have followed it. Given the care with which the panels evaluated Townsend, I deem all three to adhere to the precedent.

5.5.18 The Seventh Circuit

The Seventh Circuit considered *Townsend* in four confession cases. *Shepard's* coded three of these treatments as distinguishing it, while the other followed it. I disagree and regard them all as dismissive of *Townsend*; hence, this Circuit is not in compliance. In the first three cases (*U.S. v. Ogilvie,* 337 F.2d. 427 (1964), *VanErmen v. Burke,* 398 F.2d. 329 (1968), and *U.S. v. Pate,* 405 F.2d. 449 (1968)) the court distinguished as a means of avoiding adherence. These panels addressed *Townsend* only obliquely, viewing it as peripheral to the resolution of the controversies.

In the final Seventh Circuit case, *Weidner v. Thieret,* 932 F.2d. 626 (1991), a very lengthy opinion affirmed the district court judge while again skirting the mandate of *Townsend*. The panel had initially remanded the case to the district court to determine the voluntariness of the petitioner's confession because the "sparse factual findings failed to elucidate ... the facts underlying Weidner's [the petitioner's] confession" (at 627). The panel had suggested that the district judge secure an affidavit from the state trial judge. This he did. Weidner objected. The panel then held that "the law of the case" precluded it from revising the procedure it had originally recommended for resolving the matter. While admitting that the "difficult question is whether we erred . . . when we concluded that the hearing we instructed the district judge to hold could begin and end with 'an affidavit from the state trial judge explaining his cryptic and ambiguous ruling'" (at 631), the panel nevertheless justified its affidavit procedure as compliant with *Townsend* because "the habeas corpus statute [sic!] suggests we did not" err (at 632).

5.5.19 The Eighth Circuit

The Eighth Circuit was highly compliant in its eight decisions that treated *Townsend* in a confession context. *Shepard's* agrees, identifying seven of the cases as following *Townsend*. Although one of them does so cursorily (*Woodson v. Brewer,* 437 F.2d 1036 (1971)), care, sensitivity, and thoroughness characterizes the others, especially *Grindstaff v. Bennett,* 389 F.2d 55 (1968). Note should also be made of the compliance manifested by the panel in *Jamison v. Lockhart,* 975 F.2d 1377 (1992), which was decided after the High Court overruled *Townsend*. *Shepard's* properly identifies the treatment accorded *Townsend* in this case as questioned.

5.5.20 The Ninth Circuit

The Ninth Circuit, in its four *Townsend* decisions, is also quite compliant. *Shepard's* codes two as distinguishing and two as following, but I deem them all to be in accordance with the Court's holding in *Townsend*. *Hart v. Eyman,* 458 F.2d. 334, provides a nice example of how well-meaning circuit court judges can construe *Townsend* to come to opposite conclusions regarding its applicability. Here, both the majority and the dissent provide fair and detailed evaluations of *Townsend* in reaching their disparate results.

5.5.21 The Tenth Circuit

The Tenth Circuit treated *Townsend* only once in its confession cases. But it was extremely detailed in its consideration and application (*Church v. Sullivan,* 942 F.2d 1501 (1991)). I have read no case that exceeds the thorough, careful, and sensitive treatment afforded the precedent here.

5.5.22 The Eleventh Circuit

The Eleventh Circuit also only treated *Townsend* once in reference to a confession case. In that case, *Stinson v. Wainwright,* 710 F.2d. 743 (1983), the court summarizes *Townsend* very well and indisputably applies it fairly.

Of course, there are no cases in the D.C. circuit concerning this case as it involves only federal court treatment of state court decisions. Habeas corpus petitions in the District of Columbia do not involve considerations of federalism.

5.6 Conclusions

The most obvious and significant conclusion, which is immediately marked, is the lack of real noncompliance. While I have coded some of the *Bruton* and *Townsend* cases as "not followed," in reality their lack of enthusiasm for the Court's policy prescription is really only that: a lack of enthusiasm. It is certainly not a vendetta – all out, or even partial – against the implementation of them. Additionally, when the Courts of Appeals do somehow avoid application of a given precedent, they justify their decisions by citing reasonably persuasive reasons. Hence, my analysis is a bit artificial when it deems a certain behavior to be noncompliant. These Courts of Appeals are cognizant of the High Court's ruling, and they follow it for the most part. Their occasional deviation from that behavior, while notable, is clearly the exception even though these may well have been two cases that the lower courts did not much like.

Bruton and *Townsend* were chosen with an eye toward the analysis in Chapter 4, wherein the former was insignificant while the latter was statistically significant. Interestingly, the Courts of Appeals are seemingly less compliant with the one producing a statistical influence on their confession behavior than they are with the decision that was rendered unimportant in that analysis. One reason for this may be the way I treated *Townsend* in the last chapter. There, I used it as a decision regarding the procedure to be employed by the court in determining admissibility of a confession. The fact interacted with that decision is whether the procedure employed was fair or not.[91] However, remanding for an evidentiary hearing is only part of the Courts of Appeals' finding with respect to fair procedure. The trial court must also follow *Jackson v. Denno*, supra, and provide a hearing outside the presence of the jury in order to obtain a "yes" answer to the fairness question. This may have driven the result in the last chapter and thereby renders the two findings compatible.

Additionally, as seen by *Shepard's* coding of the Townsend cases, it is easy for the lower court to look compliant in these cases. Indeed, in coding fair procedure for Chapter 4, the lower courts' discussion was treated at face value: if it said the lower court made an adequate finding of fact, fair procedure was coded as present. Surely, given our qualitative analysis here, we might consider such compliance artificial. This is the exact contribution I hoped to make in this chapter. True, statistically the presence of fair procedure matters. But when we really dive in, we see that the Courts of Appeals may fudge the determination of the presence of this factor a bit.

In the case of *Bruton*, I do not find it particularly surprising, given my findings in this chapter, that the decision was not significant in the Courts of Appeals decision-making model presented in Chapter 4. In this chapter, I found that the Supreme Court's ruling did in fact leave substantial room for the lower courts to interpret and limit the decision and they did so in subsequent decisions over time. The Courts of Appeals employed a wide range of "valid" distinguishings when treating this case. Because I did not code for such exigencies, due to the fact that these distinguishings were too variegated and each too infrequent to admit of reliable or valid coding, these distinctions could not be included in the statistical model. Therefore, I get a non-finding with respect to the use of a codefendant's confession, when, in fact, the lower courts have been and continue to be most faithful to the precedent established in *Bruton*.

In addition, cases involving codefendant confessions were only included in the statistical model when the petitioner's confession was alleged to be involuntary. Therefore, cases resting entirely on Burton are largely absent from the statistical model. Surely, the Courts of Appeals followed the codefendant exclusion doctrine of the Supreme Court generally as demonstrated here. But, when a codefendant's confession was a factual consideration affecting the voluntariness of a confession, it may have not been so important.

Either way, a final look at Tables 5.1 and 5.2 demonstrates again the high level of compliance with Supreme Court precedent. Even when I code marginal decisions as being non-compliant, the Courts of Appeals only "disobey" the Supreme Court in less than 5% of all cases treating *Bruton* and 24% of the few cases treating *Townsend*. One should also note that noncompliance with *Townsend* is driven by two circuits. Perhaps the Fifth, because it is in the South, has somewhat divergent views. Perhaps the Seventh is different because of the ideological makeup of its panels. Either way, the high level of overall compliance cannot be gainsaid. This reaffirms our earlier findings and provides yet another example of the Courts of Appeals remaining attentive to the Supreme Court when clearly it could get away with not being so compliant. The legal, institutional, and strategic models are boosted here, but the relevance of the attitudinal model is not automatically rejected. It may well be that these panels just agree with the High Court. It is in fact the case that at least some of them were appointed by the same president, after all. But, this level of compliance surely denotes something more than mere ideological congruence. Surely it shows that the Supreme Court matters to these courts and that its constitutional position constrains it. We'll examine this institutional hypothesis in more depth in Chapter 6.

Table 5.1: Circuit Treatment of *Bruton v. United States*

Circuit	# Treated	*Shepard's* Treatment		My Coding	
		D	F	F	NF
1	5	4	1	4	1
2	18	12	6	18	0
3	0	0	0	0	0
4	7	4	3	7	0
5	37	26	11	35	2
6	18[92]	8	9	18	0
7	20	15	5	20	0
8	12[93]	6	5	12	0
9	15	10	5	14	1
10	11	10	1	10	1
11	10	5	5	9	1
D.C.	6	3	3	5	1
Total	159	103	54	152	7

Table 5.2: Circuit Treatment of *Townsend v. Sain*

Circuit	# Treated	*Shepard's* Treatment		My Coding	
		D	F	F	NF
1	1	1	0	1	0
2	3	0	3	3	0
3	4	0	4	4	0
4	3	0	3	3	0
5	10	0	10	6	4
6	3	2	1	3	0
7	4	3	1	0	4
8	8	1	7	8	0
9	4	2	2	4	0
10	1	0	1	1	0
11	1	0	1	1	0
D.C.	*Not applicable*				
Total	42	9	33	34	8

CHAPTER 6

From Judge to Justice: Institutional Effects on Judicial Decision-Making Processes

It seems that adequate evidence in previous chapters has shown that attitudes influence Courts of Appeals decision making in confession cases as does Supreme Court precedent and, to some extent, Supreme Court attitudes. Therefore, we have direct evidence of the applicability of three of the four models of decision making discussed throughout the book: the legal, the attitudinal, and the strategic. All of these seemingly apply to the Courts of Appeals to some degree. However, our evidence of new-institutional influences has been indirect at best. True, both paying heed to Supreme Court decisions and to Supreme Court ideology suggests such an influence on the Courts of Appeals, for were it free from institutional constraints it might not consider either. Indeed, the Supreme Court, which has no constraints, has been found to decide cases wholly in concert with its preferred policies (Segal and Spaeth 1993). However, to make this analysis complete, we ought to test for institutional effects more directly. This chapter does so by examining the same actors in the two different institutional settings. We have a unique opportunity to test for institutional influences here as there are several justices who started out on the Courts of Appeals bench. Indeed presidents are increasingly looking to the circuits to fill the High Bench (Goldman 1997). This allows us an opportunity to examine the same actors within varying institutional setups. This is a natural experiment in which we hold constant any potential decisional motivators that are judge-specific and vary only the institutional context in which their decisions are made. Changes in behavior can then be attributed to institutional constraints.[94]

So, in this chapter, I explore the possibility that the same judge finding himself in a different institutional context, will decide cases differently. It should be the case that the lower court judge, finding more constraints on his behavior, will decide cases with due deference to precedent and to the High Court as shown earlier. However, once set free from the bonds of the judicial hierarchy, this same judge, now a justice, should decide more in accordance with his own policy preferences, never mind any additional influences. In other words, voting on the Supreme Court should be more "sincere." In order to test for this possibility, I examine the voting and opinion writing behavior of three judges later incarnated as justices: the conservative Warren Earl Burger, the liberal Thurgood Marshall, and the hybrid Harry Andrew Blackmun. Although the confession cases in which these three participated are somewhat scarce, I think an exploration, from which we can draw some tentative conclusions, is warranted and defensible. To compliment the analysis of the confession cases, since the numbers are small, I also present their overall behavior with respect to liberal decision making and the incidence of dissent, making use of the Spaeth and Songer databases (2002, 1998 respectively). The combination of both sources of information should allow us to draw some tentative conclusions about the possibility of institutional influences on individual behavior.

6.1 The Judge Turned Justice

Warren Earl Burger served on the Court of Appeals for the District of Columbia circuit from 1956 to 1969. During that time, as can be seen by Table 6.1, he participated in the decision of 22 confession cases, 7 of which were heard by the circuit *en banc*. "As a circuit judge he attracted national attention from bench and bar for his judicial administration and for his jousts with the civil libertarians on that talented but badly divided court" (Morris 1992:104). He led the dissenters on those panels opposing the extension of rights to the criminally accused, giving preference instead to police, prosecution, and trial judges. As Chief Justice of the Supreme Court, he was the least enthusiastic on that bench to extend the civil rights decisions of the liberal and activist Warren Court. In confession cases there, he voted liberally 20% of the time, dissenting in 10% of those cases.

Table 6.2 shows data on the voting behavior of Judge/Justice Burger derived from the Songer and Spaeth datasets. The Songer dataset gives us a sample of Burger's participation while the Spaeth data provides all of them. Songer's data includes 89 participations by Burger in which an ideological direction is discernable. Of these 89, Burger voted liberally in 33, or 27%. He dissented only twice for a 2% dissent rate, which is much lower than his rate of dissent in the confession cases. Overall, Judge Burger was quite conservative, but not terribly likely to dissent. When on the High Bench, Burger remained conservative, voting liberally only 27% of the time. He dissented more often there though, voicing his opposition in 488 of 3833 cases for a 13% dissent rate.

Harry Andrew Blackmun served on the Eighth Circuit of the Court of Appeals from 1959 to 1971 when he was appointed to the High Court. While his tenure on the Court of Appeals is not often remarked upon, his voting on the Supreme Court was quite interesting. As a freshman justice, Blackmun nearly always aligned himself with the Chief Justice. So much so that the pair, Burger and Blackmun, came to be known as the "Minnesota Twins." However, as he became more comfortable on the Bench, he moved away from Burger, "becoming outspoken and explicit in his efforts to keep an increasingly conservative Court on center" (Wasby 1992:76). Even on criminal procedure, he moved away from his strongly held conservative views to become more supportive of the rights of the accused. Because I have so few of his participations in my dataset, I cannot make many broad comparisons between his tenure on the Court of Appeals and his tenure on the High Court. Nonetheless, his voting appears again to be quite consistent ideologically. In the confession cases (again, see Table 6.1), he voted liberally 25% of the time without writing one dissent, and on the Supreme Court, he voted liberally 33% of the time, again, without a dissent. His overall numbers, presented in Table 6.2, show a slightly more liberal behavior. According to the Songer database, he voted liberally in 42% of the cases in the sample, dissenting in only 3% of those. While on the High Court, he voted liberally in 41% of his cases, dissenting much more often – 16% of the time.

Thurgood Marshall served on the Second Circuit Court of Appeals from 1961 to 1965, writing several important decisions while there. In

1965, he was named the first African-American solicitor general by President Lyndon Johnson and in 1967 he became the first African-American to occupy a seat on the Supreme Court. Although we have few of his lower court opinions to examine, his voting on the Supreme Court was overwhelmingly liberal in this issue area. In my set of confession cases, Marshall *never* dissented while on the lower court (Table 6.1), even though he was often accompanied by two Republican panelists, while on the Supreme Court he dissented in fully 33% of all confession cases in which he participated. His overall numbers tell a similar story. On the Courts of Appeals, he voted liberally 55% of the time, never dissenting. On the Supreme Court, he voted liberally 64% of the time and dissented over one-third of the time.

Overall, there seems to be some evidence of an institutional constraint in these numbers. Judges on the Courts of Appeals rarely dissent. In the next section, I explore opinion writing more carefully and then draw some conclusions based on that qualitative analysis.

6.2 Exploring Decision Making and Opinion Writing From Judge to Justice

While there are very few opinions in confession cases written by judges of the Court of Appeals who are later appointed to the Supreme Court, looking directly and qualitatively at the opinions that were written by the actors in their differential roles could be quite telling. In this section I examine the language used by the judge-turned-justice to see if there are any words of reticence and then later of grandeur – that is, on the lower court, language deferential to the High Court juxtaposed with, on the Supreme Court, broadly sweeping proclamations without regard to influences other than personal policy preferences. While I have the most information for Judge/Justice Burger, I will examine all three judges, attempting to draw some conclusions about how different ideological affiliations seemingly affect role perceptions of the actor in the two institutional settings.

6.3 Judge/Justice Burger

Warren Burger participated in 22 confession cases in his tenure on the D.C. circuit. Of those 22 decisions, he only voted to exclude confessions in four cases. And notably, these four votes to exclude confessions can be readily explained while keeping to the notion that Burger was an ideological actor from the beginning. In *Naples v. U.S.*, 307 F.2d. 618, Burger concurred in the opinion of the court except for the court's mandate that the new trial be conducted by a different judge. This decision was heard *en banc*, before 6 Democratic appointees and 3 Republican appointees. The decision, as regards the confession, was unanimous, although the Republican-appointed Bastian and his Democratic counterpart Miller (who behaves as a Republican) did dissent on another aspect of the case. The fact that Burger concurred with a remand to the lower court to determine the voluntariness of the confession, then, does not seem so out of character.[95] In *Lockley v. U.S.*, 270 F.2d. 915, Burger dissented from a decision admitting a confession. However, in his dissent he did not really advocate overturning the confession. Rather, he quarrels with the court's review of the case, holding that there was no adequate basis for appellate review. Again, then, an easily understandable deviation.

In *Trilling v. U.S.*, 260 F.2d. 677, we see a somewhat constrained Warren Burger. Here, he concurs but says:

> I think the result reached by Judge Danaher is compelled by the Mallory case and therefore concur with him, but only because I conclude we are not free to do otherwise. I do this reluctantly because what Judge Prettyman [in dissent] has said makes sense and ought to be the law. The steady expansion of the meaning of 'unnecessary delay' by the courts since Rule 5(a) has been in effect suggests to me that this area of the law cannot be developed properly on a case-by-case basis, even though that is sometimes appropriate; Rule 5(a) should be re-examined by the rule making process or by Congress.

Judge Prettyman's dissent, joined by fellow-Democrat Miller[96] and the Republican-appointed Bastian, goes on at great length about what is and is not unnecessary delay, highlighting the fact that delay is not *per se* problematic. I would not categorize the opinion as being defiant of Supreme Court precedent. However, the majority here exhibits much more automatic compliance. Either way, this is a striking example of the institutional constraints placed on the Court of Appeals judge.

Clearly Burger would not decide this case in the same manner were he on the High Court, free to vote as he saw fit.

In every one of his other lower court opinions, Burger voted to allow the confession into evidence. In many of these cases, he is in the minority, as was usually the case for him on a Democratic-appointee-dominated Circuit court. In *Rettig v. United States*, 239 F.2d. 916, he argues that a suspect may not both claim she did not make the confession in question *and* claim that it was involuntary due to delay in arraignment. He cites Supreme Court cases and interprets them in doing so. In *Killough v. United States*, 315 F.2d. 241, Burger makes some bold statements in dissent. The majority in this case, again dominated by Democratic appointees, determines that a confession made a day after arraignment was the fruit of the pre-arraignment confession and thereby inadmissible. Burger is quite agitated with this ruling, saying that "The majority holding constructs an entirely new 'statute' and takes a step neither contemplated by Congress nor remotely warranted by the *Mallory* case" (at 257). He goes on,

> I find it difficult to characterize what the court does in this case. To me it is an abuse of judicial power to write what is, in effect, an amendment to Rule 5(a) because some think that Congress did not go far enough. More than that the arrogated power is exercised in a way which offends common sense. Some of the members of the court might remember that there are other branches of government at least equally qualified to frame the laws, explicitly ordained to do just that, and no less concerned than we are with individual liberty. Our task as judges, properly exercised, is a narrow one: to interpret the laws faithfully as Congress wrote them, not as we think Congress ought to have provided (at 260).

He becomes quite animated at the end of his opinion: "If it is to be the law that the courts may not use a voluntary confession, made nearly 24 hours after the judicial warning in a preliminary hearing, after time for 'deliberate reflection,' after full opportunity to secure counsel and after rejecting offers of counsel then indeed this court will have converted the shield of Rule 5(a) into a sword. What Congress clearly intended as a protection will have become a weapon of special advantage exclusively for the guilty" (at 260). As we shall see, he echoes this eloquent and passionate exposition of the duties of a judge on the High Court as well.

In *Spriggs v. United States*, 335 F.2d. 283, he dissents from a holding of unnecessary delay in arraignment because he views the delay as reasonable. In *Pea v. United States*, 397 F.2d. 627, he dissents from the majority's creation of the reasonable doubt standard in a trial judge's review of the voluntariness of a confession outside the hearing of the jury. Finally, in *Frazier v. United States*, 419 F.2d. 1161, we again find a less than deferential lower court judge, as he dissents from the majority's determination that a request by an accused not to take notes indicated a less-than-knowledgeable waiver of his rights. Burger says, first, that the *Mallory* decision "has been drawn into serious doubt by recent Congressional enactments" (at 1171). Later, discussing *Miranda,* he says that "The articulation of a stringent waiver requirement was merely a device through which the Court sought to ensure that Fifth Amendment guarantees were not unduly impaired at pre-trial interrogations. The guidelines set forth in *Miranda* were means servicing constitutionally prescribed ends; as artifices of implementation they are subordinate and only incidental to the rights they were designed to secure" (at 1172). I think this statement remarkable indeed, as a lower court judge seemingly determines for himself which portions of relevant Supreme Court precedent he will regard highly and which he will not. He goes on to chastise the rest of his panel (two Democrats) for "engag[ing] in sheer speculation of Appellant's thought processes which places a premium on the capacity of judges to probe Appellant's mind" (at 1174). I find the closing of this opinion amusing:

> Each time judges add nuances to these 'rules' we make it less likely that any police officer will be able to follow the guidelines we lay down. We are approaching the predicament of the centipede on the flypaper – each time one leg is placed to give support for relief of a leg already 'stuck,' another becomes captive and soon all are securely immobilized. Like the hapless centipede on the flypaper, our efforts to extricate ourselves from this self-imposed dilemma will, if we keep it up, soon have all of us immobilized (at 1176).

It seems that, in this case, Burger is driven purely by attitudes, and openly criticizes Supreme Court policy. As his is not the majority view, we would probably still deem this circuit as being compliant with *Miranda* and/or *Mallory* were we conducting a compliance study. However, when we switch the unit of analysis to the individual level, it may well be that we find instances of judicial disapproval of Supreme Court policy and the interpretation thereof.

Comparing the above-described behavior to Burger's behavior on the Supreme Court, we find little to denote a change in view due to the change in status. Granted, he did not participate in many cases in my dataset while on the Supreme Court. However, he did have a friendlier group of colleagues there and, therefore, was forced to dissent far less often. On the High Court, he again only voted to exclude a confession in two of ten instances. And, like those instances in which he similarly behaved on the D.C. Circuit Court of Appeal, they were cases which approximated unanimity. In *Brown v. Illinois*, 422 U.S. 590, every justice agreed that the confession be excluded from evidence, including Burger. In *Mincey v. Arizona*, 437 U.S. 385, all but Rehnquist concluded similarly. It seems that Burger is a pure ideologue. He was an ideologue on the Court of Appeals, and he remained so on the Supreme Court. Perhaps his conservative ideology accounts for this behavior. Perhaps the fact that only two others in his entire circuit consistently agreed with him (in this set of cases) might explain his exasperation with the decisions to which he was a party, and he couldn't help but dissent and dissent loudly. His circumstances may well be unique. It may be that another judge, in a more amicable environment, would play the role of faithful agent more convincingly.

Additionally, because of the differences shown in his confession voting (Table 6.1) and his overall voting (Table 6.2), we may be overstating his individualism. Indeed, in a sample of all types of cases heard, he rarely dissented while in a similar set of various issues at the Supreme Court level, he dissented 13% of the time. So, while his opinions in confession lead us to believe he was without institutional constraint, the numbers belie that claim.

6.4 Judge/Justice Blackmun

While Blackmun, like Burger, displays little behavior shift from one court to the other, as shown on Table 6.1, there is something different at work in his case. Blackmun heard only four confession cases while on the Eighth Circuit Court of Appeal. In those four cases, he was on panels with a variety of ideological compositions. He sat with a Democrat and a Republican in *Young v. United States*, 344 F.2d. 1006, and the unanimous decision, upholding use of the confession, was written by the Democrat. In another, he again sat with one Democrat and one Republican, but this time he wrote the opinion for the unanimous panel, drafting a lengthy defense of the lower court's finding of voluntariness (*Feguer v. United States*, 302 F.2d. 214). He authored another unanimous opinion for a panel consisting of himself and two Democrats, allowing another confession into evidence (*Cox v. United States*, 373 F.2d. 500). In only one decision did Blackmun vote to exclude a confession, and he wrote the opinion for a unanimous court composed of one fellow Republican and one Democrat (*Mitchell v. Stephens*, 353 F.2d. 129). He seems downright deferential to the High Court in his opinion, attempting to predict what they would do if faced with the situation therein. He opines, "But, taking into consideration all the facts, the absence of a personal expression of waiver by Mitchell, and the tremendous stake so far as he is concerned, we are not at all convinced that the Supreme Court, on this record, would uphold the district court in its determination that Mitchell had waived the coercion issue" (at 141). Perhaps none of these judges voted ideologically, or more likely, they did not need to in this set of cases because they were "cut and dry," so to speak.

When Blackmun was elevated to the High Bench, as mentioned before, he aligned himself most often with Burger until he became a bit more independent and began voting more liberally. In my dataset, I have only 9 decisions in which Blackmun participated once on the High Bench, and only one in which he actually wrote an opinion (*Brown v. Illinois*, supra). This provides very little information as to any changes from one bench to the other, just as the total lack of dissent from him decreases the utility we gain in examining his voting behavior. It is interesting to note that he does indeed appear to align himself first with Burger, and then, as time goes on, with the more liberal wing of the

Court; he is most definitely voting ideologically on the High Bench, although his ideology seemingly changed over time. But because we've so little information as to his work on the lower court, we cannot draw many conclusions. His lack of dissent, even when faced with some liberal outcomes seems to point to a seeming lack of ideological behavior. But, the cases he decided on the lower court may have just been "easier" and more clear-cut, hence avoiding the necessity for separate opinion writing. He was clearly a policy-seeker on the High Court, but his role perception while on the lower court is somewhat elusive. His overall numbers seem to connote a change (3% dissent while on the Courts of Appeals, 16% dissent while on the Supreme Court), but we cannot be sure.

6.5 Judge/Justice Marshall

The final judge-turned-justice under study is Thurgood Marshall. Again, we face data problems, having only four participations while on the Second Circuit and 15 once elevated to the Supreme Court. Compounding matters is his failure to write even in one of the four lower court decisions, while writing in only five of his 15 High Court participations. However, there remain conclusions/speculations to be drawn from his behavior on the High Bench versus his behavior on the Court of Appeals. First, while he joins each majority opinion on the lower court, whether serving with all Republicans or a Republican and a Democrat, he dissents quite often on the Supreme Court. In fact, only a few justices wrote more dissents in their tenure than he (although some wrote more in proportion to the number of their participations) (Epstein et al. 1996). In addition, he wrote opinions in one-third of his Supreme Court confession cases, although he wrote in none of the decisions while on the lower court. This may be due to the fact that some circuits of the Court of Appeals seem to assign opinions randomly (Wasby 1999) while the Supreme Court most assuredly does not (Benesh, Lowry, Sheehan, and Spaeth 1999). But nonetheless the lack of separate opinions is somewhat telling. Separate opinions in general and dissents specifically are far less frequent on the Court of Appeals than they are on the Supreme Court, which may well indicate institutional differences. The possibility nonetheless exists that Marshall simply did not deem it proper to assert his ideological bent while on the lower court, while he felt it acceptable, maybe even necessary, to do so while on the Supreme Court. In fact, in one case, he even advocated in concurrence the overruling of a two-year-old precedent (*Mincey v. Arizona*, supra) thereby showing virtually no constraint whatsoever. Even with as few cases as we have, the change in dissent rate from judge to justice is striking. Perhaps this is an indication of an institutional difference.

6.6 Conclusions and Speculations

So, what, if anything, have we learned from this? First, not all lower court judges seem to be equally constrained by the Supreme Court or by precedent. Some of the lower court judges are indeed policy driven even within the institutional constraints imposed. However, we do find some evidence that all of them are less likely to dissent while on the lower court. This is seemingly an indication that institutional constraints are at work. The exact same judge is hearing a set of similar cases in two different courts and in one, he nearly always joins the majority, while in the other he is much more likely to express disagreement. Ideologically, the voting seems to be similar across the two courts – all of the judges under study voted liberally at about the same rate on both courts. But dissent they did not. Perhaps this is driven by the decision making of the other judges on the circuits or on the High Bench. But, as seen in the qualitative section, it seems that makeup does not fully explain the differences. The institutional constraints at work here might: the mandatory and extensive docket; the rotating panels of three; the norms of behavior; and the institutional position of the court all may combine to create an environment in which judges do not feel comfortable dissenting. When they reach the High Court, those constraints disappear.

A final substantive conclusion drawn from this chapter is that judges differ. This may seem obvious, but it is worth discussing nonetheless. They differ from each other even when serving on collegial courts together. They differ in their behaviors depending upon the court on which they are currently sitting (or at least we think they do). They differ from other political actors in that their constraints are different. They differ in their perceptions of the jobs they do and the ways in which that job should be done. They differ ideologically, some finding truth in the conservative view of a given issue and others finding solace in the liberal view. They differ from themselves at a given point of time, as they mature or perhaps become more comfortable with their role. Regardless, they differ, and if we continue to do research at the aggregate level, we miss this fascinating aspect of judicial behavior. We miss the actual behavior of the judges. Therefore, let me join Gibson (1998) in advocating more research at the individual level so that we may better understand judges and better explain why they differ. For only in such an explanation and such an understanding can we get to the universal theories of judicial behavior that we all hope exist.

Table 6.1: Judge to Justice Voting Behavior in Confession Cases

	Judge Burger	Justice Burger
Number of Cases	22	10
Votes to Exclude Confessions	4	2
Percent Liberal Voting	18%	20%
Number of Dissents	8	1
Percent Dissenting	36%	10%
	Judge Blackmun	Justice Blackmun
Number of Cases	4	9
Votes to Exclude Confessions	1	3
Percent Liberal Voting	25%	33%
Number of Dissents	0	0
Percent Dissenting	0%	0%
	Judge Marshall	Justice Marshall
Number of Cases	4	15
Votes to Exclude Confessions	2	12
Percent Liberal Voting	50%	80%
Number of Dissents	0	5
Percent Dissenting	0%	33%

Table 6.2: Judge to Justice Voting Behavior in All Cases[97]

	Judge Burger	Justice Burger
Number of Cases	89	3833
Liberal Votes	33	1040
Percent Liberal Voting	37%	27%
Number of Dissents	2	488
Percent Dissenting	2%	13%
	Judge Blackmun	Justice Blackmun
Number of Cases	98	5194
Liberal Votes	41	2132
Percent Liberal Voting	42%	41%
Number of Dissents	3	839
Percent Dissenting	3%	16%
	Judge Marshall	Justice Marshall
Number of Cases	31	5155
Liberal Votes	17	3315
Percent Liberal Voting	55%	64%
Number of Dissents	0	1733
Percent Dissenting	0%	34%

CHAPTER 7

Conclusion: Faithful Agents, Ideological Actors

This book has attempted to better understand decision making in the United States Courts of Appeals, while accounting for the influence of the Supreme Court in its role as principal. Although scholarly attention is beginning to focus on these lower courts, most research in judicial politics continues to focus on the Supreme Court. However, as can be seen by mere reference to the number of unreviewed Courts of Appeals decisions, the decisions of the lower federal appellate courts are increasingly becoming final – the law of the land. Because the Supreme Court hears so few of them, it behooves us to turn our energies to understanding decision making in these increasingly important courts. This book has done that, and I think we gain some valuable insights from it. While it is focused on a certain subset of cases, and while it bears direct relevance to only one time span, I think the conclusions to be drawn from this study are not unlike those that would be drawn had we a universe of cases. Insights found here can be applied to other issue areas and to other times, and in so doing the universality of my contentions can be expressly tested. However, short of doing that, I do think it valid to draw conclusions from what we see here, noting that it is possible that not all lower court behavior is the same as that under study, but also that it is probably not all that different.

The overarching argument in the book is that the Courts of Appeals decide cases differently from the Supreme Court. While models of decision making on the High Court focus on attitudes, I attempt to use a brand of principal-agent theory that includes variables derived from all four models of judicial decision making – the legal, attitudinal, strategic, and institutional – in order to explain Courts of Appeals decision making. In order to do so, I have employed those cases involving confession, coding each as to its facts. The data were validly and reliably compiled and so the inferences drawn from them garner acceptability. In addition to a multivariate analysis, I formulated a formal model of lower court/Supreme Court interaction, assigning payoffs and calculating expected utilities. I also took some findings of interest from the quantitative analysis and looked more carefully at the reaction of the Courts of Appeals to Supreme Court decision making, reading lower court treatment of High Court policy prescriptions and deriving some other intriguing findings. Finally, I looked to the individual justices to determine whether they changed their behavior when they were elevated to the High Bench from the Courts of Appeals. Through all of these approaches, I looked for evidence of the influence of the four models of judicial decision making finding that generally attitudes matter, the law matters, Courts of Appeals judges are strategic, and Courts of Appeals judges are under institutional constraints. In other words, the model espoused here works quite well. It does indeed appear to be the case that decision making at this lower level is more complicated and additional variables are relevant. They are ideological, they are strategic, they are faithful, and they are constrained. Each chapter highlighted some aspect of that decision making and the major findings of each are summarized below.

7.1 Why Comply?

Chapter 2 highlights the attitudinal, institutional, and strategic influences on decision making. The attitudinal model is highlighted by introducing the Brehm and Gates model of principal agency in which compliance is expected only when ideological agreement is obtained. Strategic considerations come to bear on the lower courts' attention to the Supreme Court and avoidance of possible reversal, although there we see that possibility is quite rare. Finally, institutional variables are explored as constraints on behavior are discussed. Using a simplistic brand of formal theory, I found that were the lower courts to use extant data about the probability of appeal, Supreme Court review, and Supreme Court reversal, they would find that they would be better off voting their preferences without regard to Supreme Court prescription on the matter. However, for some reason, they still comply. This leads me to believe that when it comes to the principal-agency relationship between the lower courts and the Supreme Court, the High Court exerts an immeasurable influence on the lower courts. That influence, I conclude, is one of moral authority. Scholars have discussed this moral authority before (Baum 1998:242-3), (Canon and Johnson say the lower courts have an obligation to comply (1999:35)) concluding that it certainly plays a role in lower court compliance with Supreme Court policy prescriptions, but the difficulty lies in measuring that impact explicitly. Most certainly, a High Court lacking in authority would gain but little compliance, and so it is logical that the widespread compliance found here and elsewhere can be attributed to said authority. The proof of the existence of such a force is as follows: given that it is rarely in the interest of the lower court to comply with Supreme Court precedents, while nonetheless recognizing that the Supreme Court's decisions do matter greatly to the lower courts, the inference that moral authority must be driving compliance can be validly drawn. The impetus to comply comes from what the Supreme Court *is* rather than what it *does*. No longer does loyalty seem to be irrational. Rather, it is deemed such a part of the culture and socialization of these judges that there is very little question when a choice exists between one's own policy goals and Supreme Court precedent. This is the very definition of an institutional constraint. However, this does not completely preclude a lower court judge voting his or her own attitudes. It merely means that if they do, they must find a way to make that decision at least *look* compliant. In Chapter 5, I show some of the ways that the lower courts do that, while still maintaining that compliance is the norm.

7.2 Decision Making in the Courts of Appeals

The conclusion that the High Court matters because of what it is, not what it does, still leaves the question of how the lower court decides cases. Does the lower court merely decide as the Supreme Court would have it decide, no questions asked? In Chapter 4 we found that, while Court policy does matter to the lower courts, they retain their autonomy and still vote at least partially in accordance with their own individual policy preferences. The lower courts pay heed to precedent; they take note of Supreme Court membership; *and* they vote their attitudes. Again, we find evidence of the influence of the legal, the strategic (or institutional) and the attitudinal, respectively. It has long been argued that, while the Supreme Court decides almost solely according to the policy preferences of its members, perhaps with some strategic interaction as well, lower court judges, finding themselves in a different institutional setting, necessarily must take into account other factors and other actors. In so doing, the lower court judges' calculus is much more complicated than that of Supreme Court justices. While there are undoubtedly judges, even on the lower courts, who vote their attitudes consistently (as seen in part in Chapter 6), as a whole the lower court judges need to be less personally preferential than are the High Court justices. They do have an obligation to decide cases in line with the Supreme Court's jurisprudence, and when in doubt as to the High Court's preference, it may even be argued that they should attempt to anticipate how the High Court would decide (Gruhl 1980). Either way, the lower court judge is not completely a free agent, and so the Court's ideological composition as well as many of the Court's precedents matter to these lower court judges. Also notable is the lack of real difference among the circuits in their decision making, at least insofar as the confession cases are concerned. Only the D.C. and the Tenth Circuits differ considerably from the others. The D.C. Circuit's jurisdiction and caseload differ from the other circuits, however, and so this seeming incongruity is probably the result of the circuit's docket rather than a differential decision-making calculus. The Tenth, with its different history and criminal caseload, probably also has some different norms. Both, however, remain largely compliant.

7.3 But, Is It Complete Compliance?

While we find much evidence that the lower court does in fact comply with Supreme Court precedent – and other studies have found similarly – it is necessary to note that the lower courts needn't completely thwart

Supreme Court precedent in order to be less than compliant with its decisions. In fact, as discussed, there are a number of things a lower court can do, short of defiance, in order to limit the effect of an unliked Supreme Court precedent. In Chapter 5, I examined cases qualitatively to look for creative noncompliance. Using one Supreme Court precedent that was determined to be significantly related to lower court decision making in Chapter 4 (*Townsend v. Sain*) and one that was not (*Bruton v. United States*), I examined lower court treatment of Supreme Court precedent. I found substantial compliance with both decisions, and possibly more compliance with the one that was *not* significant. Overall, the Courts of Appeals complied in 95% of the cases treating *Bruton* and in 76% of those treating *Townsend.* While there were occasional strained distinguishings and a couple of cases that seemingly violated the spirit of the Supreme Court pronouncement, the lower courts generally comply. There are indeed cases in which distinguishing the case from the Court's precedent is valid; so this type of behavior is not automatically problematic. Only occasionally were these distinguishings unduly artificial.

7.4 Different Courts = Different Justices?

Finally, in Chapter 6, I discuss the possibility that the lower court judge, once elevated to the Supreme Court and given the freedom to make decisions according to his attitudes, will in fact decide cases differently. In other words, not satisfied with the indirect tests for institutional constraints presented in earlier chapters, I test for institutional constraints directly. In order to investigate this possibility, I explore the decision making of the three judges-turned-justice who served a significant time on both courts: Justices Burger, Blackmun, and Marshall. In that qualitative look at their jurisprudence, I found some indications for each of them that institutions matter; that is, each was constrained in some way while on the lower court. They maintain their ideological bent, but their dissent behavior is certainly constrained on the lower court. This provides some indication of institutional differences and the effects thereof.

7.5 Unanswered Questions, and Directions for Future Research

Overall, we find a highly compliant lower court that, while deciding cases attentive to the policy prescriptions and attitudinal predispositions of the Supreme Court, is still able to incorporate its policy preferences into its decision making. Judges on the lower courts, while more constrained than those on the High Court, may nonetheless decide cases in substantially the same manner on each. However, they are much freer to do so on the High Court as they obviously needn't fear being overruled. In addition, on the Supreme Court, they also have at least some say in the types of cases they and the Court will hear, while those serving on the Courts of Appeals must hear them all. Attitudinal theory remains relevant as do legal, strategic, and institutional factors. Though the judges are faithful legal agents, working under institutional constraints, they are also strategic and ideological actors.

However, questions remain with respect to lower court decision making. First, exactly how much do differences in decisions account for differences in outcome? That is, does the finding that the lower court overturns proportionately far fewer confessions than the Supreme Court mean anything substantively, or does that finding merely suggest that the lower court is hearing claims that are less meritorious than those heard by the Supreme Court? Since every defendant has the opportunity to appeal his or her case to the Court of Appeals and that court must hear that claim, the possibility of frivolous suits making it to that court are far higher than the possibility that they are heard by the Supreme Court. It would be a relevant and useful endeavor to examine exactly what the differential docket of the lower court means to its decision making. Do workload considerations constrain the lower court to decide in accordance with the Supreme Court simply because it is easier (i.e., less time-consuming) to do so? Are the cases so often without merit that the appeal to the Court of Appeals actually means very little, as the district court determination is so often upheld there? Once we develop methods for empirically analyzing the substantive merit of the cases appealed to the Courts of Appeals and determine exactly what impact that has on decision making, we will have more confidence in our finding that the lower court does indeed decide cases differently from the Supreme Court.

The second unanswered question refers to the actual role of ideology in the lower courts. We find that when we add a variable for ideology into a model of lower court decision making, that variable is significant; nonetheless, exactly what role ideology plays in lower court decision making remains unknown. Is it deterministic as it is in the Supreme Court, or is it merely contributory, as our results suggest? Does it explain separate opinions on the lower courts as it does on the Supreme Court; e.g., do dissenters dissent for ideological reasons, or are there other constraints?[98] Do the ideological predispositions of the judges of the Court of Appeals change over time, or are they relatively stable? Finally, are there further strategic considerations here, as exist at the Supreme Court level? What is it about the Court of Appeals as an institution that fosters or hinders such strategic interaction?

The third inadequately answered question is that contained in Chapter 6; institutional effects on decision making. An individual-level analysis such as this is highly desirable and eminently useful, provided it be conducted at a more rigorous level. Here I am only able to glean some vaguely interesting patterns of differential or similar behavior. A larger scale analysis would lend much to the knowledge we have about the effects of institutional constraints on decision making, and this type of study is something that should occupy a high place on future research agendas.

Finally, do my results extend to other subject areas at other points in time? Has the lower court become more ideological over time? Are differences in decision making dependent on the subject matter under consideration? Do different parties draw a different type of response from these judges? While some of these matters are being addressed by scholars in the field, it remains important to recognize that this is but one study at one point in time using one set of cases. In order to fully understand the range and depth of influences on lower court decision making, we must continue with this sort of research until we have the knowledge of these lower federal courts (and state supreme courts and trial courts and courts of other nations) that we currently have of the

United States Supreme Court. Arguably, these courts are the most important. In the vast majority of cases, they authoritatively prescribe the law of the land. If we are to understand the impact of the judiciary on our lives, and on democracy in general, we necessarily must turn away from our one unique (yet important) United States Supreme Court, and begin to come to a theory and an understanding of courts in general. In so doing, our knowledge will become as broad and deep and influential as it possibly can be, thereby maximizing our contribution to society.

Endnotes

[1]Segal and Spaeth also mention the fact that electoral sanctions exist for some lower court judges which do not exist for Supreme Court justices, but this does not apply to the Courts of Appeals.

[2]The desirable traits for an organization in the social choice literature include: 1) nonrestriction of individual preferences; 2) unanimity, or Pareto optimality; 3) independence of irrelevant alternatives; and 4) transitivity (Miller and Moe, 1986:178). Because these are such basic requirements for an organization, it may be surprising that the authors find that only in dictatorship are all of these conditions met. By mentioning the fact that hierarchies cannot achieve all four conditions simultaneously, I attempt to make the case that individual preferences will be restricted in order for the judiciary to function.

[3]The total cost of agency to the principal, then, is "...the sum of the investments made in limiting shirking plus the costs associated with remaining or residual shirking" (Eggertson 1990:44).

[4]Some ways to deal with this agency relationship include Stevens' "screening and selection of agents," "contract design," "monitoring and reporting," and "institutional checks" (Stevens 1993:284-287). Screening of agents during the selection process can solve the adverse selection problem, and contract design can make certain behaviors unacceptable. Monitoring can take place via police patrol or fire alarm type oversight, the choice between which reflects the cost a principal will accept in monitoring its agents. From the names of these two types of principal oversight, one should be able to ascertain that the police-patrol type is much more costly than the fire-alarm oversight type (Shepsle and Bonchek 1997). Stevens discusses the ability of other institutions to play a role in the effectuation of policy as a solution to this agency problem.

[5]The moral hazard problem does continue to plague the Supreme Court, however, as its attempt to oversee the lower courts is limited to those cases which are appealed by the litigants. This leaves most jurisprudence outside the review of the Court. This will be discussed further.

[6]Here, though, one may find cases in which the Court extends or restricts jurisdiction. However, these extensions or changes are still subject to

legislation that could reverse them, since Congress determines all of the lower courts' jurisdiction, as well as virtually all of the Supreme Court's.

[7]The author thanks Dave Rohde for pointing this out.

[8]It would be interesting, however, to determine in which types of cases the probability of review and reversal is highest, and then determine whether or not the lower court judges perceive these differences. If so, and shirking on those likely to be reviewed cases declined, support for the principal-agent theory could be shown, while still recognizing that the Court does not provide substantial inducements to get the lower court to comply with its preferences.

[9]Responsiveness should be here distinguished from congruence, as responsiveness implies that as the Supreme Court modifies its doctrine, so the appeals court modifies its doctrine in the same direction. Congruence, on the other hand, implies that an appeals court and the Supreme Court, given the same facts, would decide the case in the same way. Congruence is time dependent and specific to a given decision, while responsiveness is more a measure of trends and the propensity of the lower court to follow the Supreme Court ideologically. The former leaves minimal room for the lower court to exercise attitudes, while the latter does afford some leeway.

[10]Of course, this could mean a substantial broadening of the doctrine enunciated by the Court as well, but I would consider this as following the Court enthusiastically, contrary to Reid's conclusions (1987).

[11]This notion of hierarchical theory, as well as that espoused by Songer, Segal and Cameron (1994), or the organizational model advocated by Baum (1976), is not the same as the oft-criticized earlier hierarchy theory as mentioned, for example, in Richardson and Vines (1970). The earlier work was far more rigid in its prescription of the supremacy of the High Court than is the current model.

[12]Richardson and Vines (1970) offer a cute illustration: "The popular sentiment that one will appeal a case 'all the way to the Supreme Court' is somewhat of a popular myth to the extent that it symbolized the court's appellate function. A more realistic and accurate statement would be the assertion that the case will be appealed 'all the way to the Court of Appeals'" (149).

[13]Several studies add communication or knowledge of decisions as a prerequisite to compliance (Canon and Johnson 1999; Tarr 1977). The Courts of Appeals have no problem in this regard. Either the judges keep

up with the decisions of the High Court themselves or they are briefed about them by the lawyers who appear before them or by the law clerks with which they are provided (Canon and Johnson 1999; Tarr 1977).

[14]It seems, though, that the D.C. Circuit has had its share of skirmishes with the High Court (Belcaster 1992; Murphy 1959).

[15]The ordering of the actors' preferences.

[16]"The sum across all possible outcomes of a decider's utility for each possible outcome times the probability of that outcome's occurring if a given action is chosen" (Morrow 1994:350).

[17]Recall that "leisure shirking" refers to not working for the sole purpose of increased leisure; e.g., the preference of doing nothing to doing work in accord with the principal's action.

[18]Lower courts are increasingly falling behind due to an overwhelming workload. According to Ralph Mecham, the Director of the Administrative Office of the U. S. Courts, "The demands placed on United States judges today are staggering. Jurists at virtually every level of our federal system are facing a greater number of cases, which involve increasingly complex issues, explore novel areas of the law, and consume a larger portion of their time" (Redmond 1996:1).

[19]Recall that "dissent shirking" refers to avoidance of work due to ideological differences between the principal and the agent.

[20]The author thanks Scott Gates for help in formulating the analysis in this chapter.

[21]Payoffs were determined by adding and subtracting the relevant considerations, and then ranking the outcomes. For example, the payoffs for the Court of Appeals associated with Not follow, No appeal = Policy – Leisure – Stare Decisis – Role + Supervision (no negative costs due to supervision) = 8 (best outcome). The payoff for the Supreme Court for the same outcome is –Policy – Power + Supervision (no cost of supervision) = 1 (worst outcome).

[22]It is duly noted that this is not a true formalization of the relationship under study. Indeed, I should allow the unknowns to vary and determine under what circumstances the lower court might shirk, work, or sabotage and the Supreme Court might monitor. However, I choose here to simply demonstrate how, with current known probabilities, the Court of Appeals

may be reacting to the possibility of Supreme Court review and reversal. Assuming, then, that actual probabilities are what the lower court uses in determining its behavior and that the lower court believes those probabilities are unchangeable, these results follow. Those assumptions are tenuous, of course. For a more formal model of this relationship, see Benesh 2002.

[23]One could also substitute only two of the three unknowns finding tipping points for the others in order to further understand lower court considerations in the decision to follow. In so doing, however, I find that the tendency to not follow is so strong that the lower court will never switch from non-compliance to compliance (the value for the tipping point in all cases is negative). It seems that the Supreme Court, therefore, should theoretically always face the problem of noncompliance.

[24]373 U.S. 503 (1963)

[25]Generally, the influence of facts on outcomes is seen as a legalistic consideration (Segal 1984). However, it is most likely the case that judges will have attitudes about these facts as well as attitudes about their desired outcomes. Therefore, while the facts are used here as an indicator of precedent and hence the influence of the Supreme Court on Courts of Appeals decision making, one should note that the ideological predispositions of the Court will impact the facts deemed important, as seen in the next section.

[26]"Third degree" may be defined as: "the employment of methods which inflict suffering, physical or mental, upon a person in order to obtain information about a crime" (Stephens, 1973:10).

[27]Bureau v. McDowell, 156 U.S. 465, 477 (1921)

[28]Brown v. Mississippi, 297 U.S. 278 (1936)

[29]309 U.S. at 241 (1940)

[30]McNabb v. U.S. 318 U.S. 332 (1943) and Mallory v. U.S. 354 U.S. 449 (1957)

[31]Justice Black even advocated a standard of "inherent coerciveness" (in Ashcraft v. Tennessee, 322 U.S. 143 (1944)) which would treat any interrogation as suspect because of the intrinsic element of police control. Because of its radical nature, this standard did not receive the Court's blessing for quite some time (Stephens 1973).

[32]318 U.S. at 347

[33]While Mallory did outlaw delay in arraignment solely for interrogation purposes, it did not indicate how much leeway the police would have when the arrest took place at a time when no magistrate was available for arraignment. This, of course, led to much activity in the lower federal courts.

[34]Stephens (1973:85-89) gives a good account of the opposition the Court encountered.

[35]357 U.S. 433 (1958)

[36]Rogers v. Richmond, 365 U.S. 534, at 540 (1961)

[37]Malloy v. Hogan, 378 U.S. 1 (1964)

[38]367 U.S. 643 and 378 U.S. 478, respectively

[39]384 U.S. 436 (1966)

[40]Ibid at 475

[41]394 U.S. 478 (1969)

[42]401 U.S. 222

[43]Id. at 476

[44]373 U.S. 503 (1963)

[45]Lee v. Mississippi, 332 U.S. 742 (1948)

[46]Payne v. Arkansas, 356 U.S. 560 (1958)

[47]Turner v. Pennsylvania, 338 U.S. 62 (1949)

[48]Davis v. North Carolina, 384 U.S. 737 (1966)

[49]Fay v. Noia, 372 U.S. 391 (1963), Escobedo v. Illinois, 378 U.S. 478 (1964), Miranda v. Arizona, 384 U.S. 436 (1966)

[50]Culombe v. Connecticut, 367 U.S. 568 (1961); Gallegos v. Colorado, 370 U.S. 49 (1962); Spano v. New York, 360 U.S. 315 (1959)

[51]Then Judge Cardoza in People v. Defore, 150 N.E. 585 at 587 (1927).

[52]See Stephens (1973:165-200) for references to a number of such studies.

[53]I do employ Shepard's in a subsequent chapter, however, and deem that there Songer's criticism is lacking in force. He does have a point, however, where the selection of cases for this type of analysis is concerned. If I were to rely on the Court of Appeals to cite Supreme Court precedent, I would miss instances wherein they merely cite none or where they cite their own cases as precedent, thereby potentially missing important realizations of Court of Appeals non-compliance, although some studies have found this to be the exception rather than the rule (Benesh and Reddick 2002).

[54]The analysis begins with the Vinson Court because that is the earliest Court for which we have substantial data collection. The analysis ends with Stewart's resignation in 1981. The law of confession was largely settled by that time. Hence, I end my analysis there.

[55]The facts he deems relevant to decision making include prior justification of the search, the nature of the search, and the exceptions to the probable cause and warrant requirements. Within each of these areas, he identifies specific relevant facts.

[56]I code these facts directly from the opinion of the given court under study, accepting the decision of the lower court wherever the subjective facts were in dispute. The Supreme Court regularly iterates that it "...accept[s] [the lower court's] judgement insofar as facts upon which conclusion must be reached are in dispute" (Gallegos v. Nebraska, 342 U.S. 55, at 61), as does the Courts of Appeals: "This court thus accepts and adopts the state trial court's findings of facts...[We] should not disturb the state court's findings absent convincing testimony that the factual determination was erroneous" 413 F.2d. 459, at 461). It is only their appraisal thereof which may differ. As an additional check on the possibility that the appeals court is ignoring facts to obtain their preferred outcome, I code for factual disagreement among the majority and the court's dissenter(s). Such disagreement may signal a court majority that is playing loose with the facts.

[57]Here, I use the word "overturn" loosely. What we are actually measuring again is whether the court accepts the confession as is. The Court may well remand the case to the lower court for further proceedings without

overturning it explicitly. In such cases, the outcome is coded as overturning, which we will use here to mean "unacceptable in its current state."

[58]I have included an "other" category because some cases involve unique defendants and the unique characteristics of those defendants do indeed affect the determination of confession's admissibility. Examples include a mother of several small children, a drug addict, a defendant with high blood pressure, a defendant who was ill, and a defendant who was very slight of build. Many of these defendant characteristics have been noted to increase the level of coercion likely to have been present during the interrogation.

[59]According to Perry (1991), the Supreme Court often takes cases to reverse them. The Courts of Appeals do not seem to behave similarly (see, e.g., Songer, Sheehan, and Haire 2001).

[60]Source: West's American Digest System. Various Dates. St. Paul: West Publishing Company.

[61]517.1 through 517.3 appear only in and after the Ninth Decennial, which covers dates from 1981 - 1986.

[62]This list merely reproduces Kort's Table 1 (1963:137). I have added to and subtracted from it, as Table 3.3 shows.

[63]One could argue that this integrated model should also include some external influences on the Courts of Appeals. However, because said external influences have not been adequately studied for these lower courts and because measures of public opinion or "mood" are elusive at best, I have decided not to include those potential factors here. Their applicability to decision making in the lower courts, however, could be explored in future research.

[64]As noted by Lindquist (2001), it is unwarranted to assume that these circuits are mere members of a larger court and so may be treated as one unit of analysis. Indeed, it might be argued that the institutional differences among the circuits may preclude validly grouping them. In order to determine whether circuits are too different even to treat as a single court, I ran a simple, one-way ANOVA. (One of my graduate students, Deborah Knudson, conceived this test.) In so doing, I find no appreciable differences in the mean liberal proportion of cases per year per circuit ($F = 0.905$, sig=0.537). Therefore, it seems defensible to lump the circuits as one court while still being able to test for differences in decision making

models across circuits. None of them are so deviant as to preclude their inclusion in the analysis.

[65]Of course, it is possible that the lower courts anticipate decisions by the Supreme Court (see, e.g., Reddick and Benesh 2000), or perhaps, in deciding a case without a Supreme Court policy prescription, they consider the presence or absence of a given fact to be important.

[66]Because I was concerned that using the year of decision in the Supreme Court would prove to be too gross, because the trials from which the appellant is appealing to the Courts of Appeals may have been heard before the relevant Supreme Court precedent, I also ran the analysis with this dummy lagged at one year. This did not change the results appreciably and so I employ the current measure.

[67]We have a huge number of potential independent variables here due to the incremental decision making of the Supreme Court in this area. Because of this, choices have to be made over which variables to include and which to leave out. Initially, I ran an omnibus model in which all facts were included. This proved problematic because many of the facts under consideration predict a given outcome perfectly. This results because in every case wherein the variable takes on a specific value, the dependent variable is the same. They include the following: physical coercion, length of detention, no place of detention, relays, place of interrogation, no codefendent confession, no prior coerced confession, and no race. Thus, for example, in every single case in which there is some physical coercion, the court excludes the confession. Such a variable cannot be included in the model because it has no variance. It is important to note the large impact it has on the court's decision even though we cannot explicitly model it, however. Interestingly, two of the aforementioned perfect predictors are those facts for which the Supreme Court heard a substantial number of cases (race and police relays). This provides some additional evidence of the differential strength hypothesis. After those variables were purged, an extensive set of likelihood ratio tests were conducted to determine whether insignificant variables might also be removed. Likelihood ratio tests assure that the exclusion of those variables not providing a statistically significant impact did not harm the results. In other words, exclusion of variables was based on their overall theoretical contribution to the model rather than their mere statistical insignificance (Granato 1991). This final model, more parsimonious than the one including all facts identified, provided the best fit.

[68]The scores ranged from –0.12 to 0.66. Thus, I deemed any Courts with a mean ideology score greater than 0.5 to be liberal, and less than 0.5 to be conservative. This seemingly fits the distribution of scores well, and is a

conservative measure of this concept thereby increasing confidence in any obtained significance.

[69]I conducted several diagnostic tests on this model to determine its robustness. First, I tested for multicollinearity examining the correlation matrix. None approached 0.7, so I deem multicollinearity to be absent. Second, I tested for omitted variable bias using the RESET test, finding that including the dependent variable on the right hand side did nothing to the estimates, and its coefficient was insignificant. Third, I tested for heteroskedasticity among circuits by running a heteroskedastic probit. I conclude therefrom that heteroskedasticity is not a problem, as the term for variance was insignificant. Finally, I tested for influential cases using Cook's D. While there were a few influential cases, their inclusion does not significantly alter results. We can have much confidence in these data, then, and in the results obtained via this estimation.

[70]There is some debate over the usefulness of the R^2 statistic, or coefficient of determination. For example, Achen (1982) argues that, since R^2 is dependent upon the variation in the independent variables and that variance is clearly a function of the sample, it makes little sense to attribute to its value a measure of the strength of the relationship between the independent and dependent variables. King concurs (1986). More problems occur when using the pseudo-R^2 as we are forced to here due to our method (probit), because that measure is calculated differently depending upon the statistical package being utilized. It is better, when running probit or other maximum likelihood techniques, to rely upon the percent correctly predicted, which will also be duly reported (Hagle and Mitchell 1992).

[71]I also ran the facts established in the various precedents without reference to the year in which they were decided in order to determine whether it was merely the fact that was signficantly related to the treatment of the confession or rather the Supreme Court pronouncement on the matter mattered. I find that, indeed, the fact is relevant regardless of the time span. However, upon further investigation, I realized that most of my observations are post-1960 which is around the time most of the precedent-setting cases I discuss were decided (only 78 of the 563, or 14%, were decided before 1960). Therefore, we can confidently attribute the significance of these facts to the Supreme Court's decisions.

[72]Results of these estimations available upon request.

[73]Model fit statistics are as follows: Wald Chi2 (35) = 205.22; Prob > Chi2 = 0.0000; Pseudo R2 = 0.7076; Percent Correctly Predicted = 94.06%; Reduction in Error = 73.3%

[74]Predicted probabilities are calculated with all other variables at their mean.

[75]In the interest of space, coefficients and significance levels are not reported for the other independent variables as they change little from those reported in Table 4.3.

[76]In the interest of space, coefficients and significance levels are not reported for the other independent variables as they change little from those reported in Table 4.3.

[77]Brown v. Board of Education, 347 U.S. 483 (1954).

[78]I, of course, offer no normative argument as to the benefits or detriments of vertical stare decisis.

[79]And theirs is a study of trial courts.

[80]Amar, quoting another legal scholar, said that perhaps an unhappy lower court judge should (again, we do not deal in normatives here) say to the higher court: "Go ahead, make my day: reverse me. You're wrong about the Constitution. You've taken your oath of office, but that's no excuse for my violating mine. I'm going to follow my oath of office and decide the Constitution correctly as I understand it. If you don't like it, take cert" (1994:41). While admittedly a bit drastic, it does present an argument seemingly congruent to that of some of the state court justices cited above and elsewhere.

[81]In this case, a person, suffering from some sort of mental incapacitation, attempted to render his voluntary statement to a policeman involuntary due simply to his mental state. The Court said that coercive police activity is a necessary predicate to finding a confession involuntary. It distinguished Townsend, where the petitioner was given a truth serum, from the case at bar because in Townsend there was evidence of police coercion. Here, there was none.

[82]Shepard's lists Idaho v. Wright, 497 U.S. 805 as distinguishing Bruton, but I see it as following the holding in Bruton.

[83]I have necessarily excluded unpublished decisions (for problems inherent in this exclusion see Songer and Davis 1989; Pacelle and Baum 1992). Upon a quick reading of such cases, there appears to be no systematic bias resulting from this exclusion. (A LEXIS search was

conducted using the name of the Supreme Court decision and the word "unpublished.")

[84]Cases were identified as per Brenner and Spaeth 1995.

[85]Some of the overruling and overruled decisions had no key numbers in common, as the Key Number System has evolved over the years, adding some keys and removing others. In these cases, we chose key numbers from the overruling decision which pertained to the basis upon which the Court was altering its prior decision.

[86]Additionally, my analysis in Chapter 4 does not rely in any way on Shepard's and so should have uncovered this type of noncompliance if it existed, at least if it was in any way systematic. It uncovered none.

[87]This is admittedly a subjective exercise. However, it is quite easy to determine whether a true distinguishing or a mere excuse is present in a given case (Benesh and Reddick 2002). In either event, I fully discuss any case deemed to be noncompliant so the reader can readily make a judgment as to the decisions made in coding these cases.

[88]I eliminated all cases containing a "neutral" treatment from Shepard's (e.g., explained, harmonized, or cited), as I am not concerned with said cases. I also eliminated all cases with a reference to the Supreme Court precedent only within either a different opinion (e.g., a concurrence) or a dissenting opinion. Finally, I eliminated any case that was not based upon a coerced confession.

[89]As mentioned previously, Benesh and Reddick (2002) tested for the validity of *Shepard's* "followed" coding, as did Spriggs and Hansford (2000). Both found that Shepard's designation comported with standard definitions of "following."

[90]The Third Circuit did not treat *Bruton* in any of its confession cases.

[91]This is a subjective determination to be sure. However, the two prerequisites for fairness (a *Jackson* hearing and a *Townsend* consideration of habeas corpus cases) were used in this determination.

[92]*Shepard's* codes one case as limiting *Bruton*.

[93]*Shepard's* codes one case as limiting *Bruton*.

[94]Of course, we cannot render the decisions equivalent; so while it is probably the case that differences derive from context, the different cases heard by each court may in themselves cause different decisions. In other words, if the decisions at the Courts of Appeals are largely frivolous, even the most liberal judge will vote to exclude. Therefore, in discussing results here, we should bear in mind the potential that any differences in decision making found to exist may derive from differences in cases heard.

[95]When an ideologue joins a unanimous court in the resolution of some issue, it seems safe to assume that the case was "easy" or straightforward. Even the attitudinal model does not fully explain unanimous decisions. [While this common-sense explanation is probably persuasive, there is seemingly a research question to explore: why are there unanimous decisions?] I think that viewing them as noncontroversial cases explains the seemingly incongruity with a model that emphasizes preferences over all other considerations.

[96]While Wilbur K. Miller was indeed appointed by a Democrat, his voting behavior is much more consistent with that of a conservative.

[97]Data on judges' behavior on the Courts of Appeals from the Songer database (1998); data on justices' behavior on the Supreme Court from the Spaeth database (2002).

[98]One such constraint immediately comes to mind: do district court judges, sitting by designation on a certain panel of the circuit court, behave differently from those on the court full-time? Are there fewer dissents registered by said justices; fewer majority opinions written? Does this judge face the additional constraint of being an outsider, or of a lower position? These are interesting questions that the research has not yet addressed.

Table of Cases

Courts of Appeals Cases

Allison v. Holman 326 F.2d. 294 (1963)
Bowden v. Francis 733 F.2d. 740 (1984)
Burns v. Beto 371 F.2d. 598 (1967)
Cargill v. Turpin 120 F.3d. 1366 (1997)
Childs v. Cardwell 452 F.2d. 541 (1971)
Church v. Sullivan 942 F.2d. 1501 (1991)
Close v. U.S. 450 F.2d. 152 (1971)
Cockrell v. Oberhauser 413 F.2d. 256 (1969)
Cox v. U.S. 373 F.2d. 500 (1967)
Dempsey v. Wainwright 471 F.2d. 604 (1973)
Duggar v. U.S. 434 F.2d. 345 (1970)
Edwards v. Garrison 529 F.2d. 1374 (1975)
Evans v. Buchanan 256 F.2d. 688 (1958)
Farmer v. Kropp 445 F.2d. 5 (1971)
Federated Mutual Implement and Hardware Insurance Co. v. Fairfax Equipment Company, Inc. 261 F.2d. 207 (1958)
Feguer v. U.S. 302 F.2d. 214 (1962)
Folston v. Allsbrook 691 F.2d. 184 (1982)
Frazier v. U.S. 419 F.2d. 1161 (1969)
Gotcher v. Beto 444 F.2d. 696 (1971)
Grieco v. Meachum 533 F.2d. 713 (1976)
Grindstaff v. Bennett 389 F.2d. 55 (1968)
Hart v. Eyman 458 F.2d. 334 (1972)
Hoover v. Beto 467 F.2d. 516 (1972)
Jamison v. Lockhart 975 F.2d. 1377 (1992)
Killough v. U.S. 315 F.2d. 241 (1962)
LaFrance v. Bohlinger 499 F.2d. 29 (1974)
Lockley v. U.S. 270 F.2d. 915 (1959)
McHenry v. U.S. 420 F.2d. 927 (1970)
McMillin v. Beto 447 F.2d. 453 (1971)
Migliore v. U.S. 409 F.2d. 786 (1969)
Miller v. Cox 457 F.2d. 700 (1972)
Mitchell v. Stephens 353 F.2d. 129 (1965)

Naples v. U.S. 307 F.2d. 618 (1962)
Pea v. U.S. 397 F.2d. 627 (1967)
Randolph v. Parker 575 F.2d. 1178 (1978)
Rettig v. U.S. 239 F.2d. 916 (1956)
Rios-Ramirez v. U.S. 403 F.2d. 1016 (1968)
Roberts v. U.S. 416 F.2d. 1216 (1969)
Rogers v. McMackin 884 F.2d. 252 (1989)
Santoro v. U.S. 402 F.2d. 920 (1968)
Spriggs v. U.S. 335 F.2d. 283 (1964)
Stinson v. Wainwright 710 F.2d. 743 (1983)
Tasby v. U.S. 451 F.2d. 394 (1971)
Thomas v. U.S. 409 F.2d. 730 (1969)
Trilling v. U.S. 260 F.2d. 677 (1958)
U.S. v. Akers et al. 542 F.2d. 770 (1976)
U.S. v. Arambula-Ruiz 987 F.2d. 599 (1993)
U.S. v. Arias 984 F.2d. 1139 (1993)
U.S. v. Barragan 453 F.2d. 386 (1971)
U.S. v. Burroughs 650 F.2d. 595 (1981)
U.S. v. Burroughs 935 F.2d. 292 (1991)
U.S. v. Castro 413 F.2d. 891 (1969)
U.S. v. Castro 596 F.2d. 674 (1979)
U.S. v. Coppola 788 F.2d. 303 (1986)
U.S. v. Cox 449 F.2d. 679 (1971)
U.S. v. Crockett 813 F.2d. 1310 (1987)
U.S. v. Danzey 594 F.2d. 905 (1979)
U.S. v. Donner et al. 497 F.2d. 184 (1974)
U.S. v. Espericueta-Reyes 631 F.2d. 616 (1980)
U.S. v. Follette 430 F.2d. 1055 (1970)
U.S. v. Fountain 449 F.2d. 629 (1971)
U.S. v. Gibson 416 F.2d. 326 (1969)
U.S. v. Gonzales 749 F.2d. 1329 (1984)
U.S. v. Grant 549 F.2d. 942 (1977)
U.S. v. Grillo 527 F.2d. 1344 (1979)
U.S. v. Gurule 437 F.2d. 239 (1970)
U.S. v. Hoffa 402 F.2d. 380 (1968)
U.S. v. Jackson et al. 482 F.2d. 1167 (1973)
U.S. v. Jimenez 780 F.2d. 975 (1986)
U.S. v. Johnson 478 F.2d. 1129 (1973)
U.S. v. Kelley et al. 526 F.2d. 615 (1975)
U.S. v. Kendricks 623 F.2d. 1165 (1980)
U.S. v. Kreiser 15 F.3d. 635 (1994)
U.S. v. LaVallee 415 F.2d. 150 (1969)
U.S. v. Littman 421 F.2d. 981 (1970)
U.S. v. Maddox 492 F.2d. 104 (1974)
U.S. v. Mancusi 441 F.2d. 1073 (1971)
U.S. v. Maurice 416 F.2d. 234 (1969)

U.S. v. McManus 560 F.2d. 747 (1977)
U.S. v. Montgomery 582 F.2d. 514 (1978)
U.S. v. Ogilvie 337 F.2d. 427 (1964)
U.S. v. Pate 405 F.2d. 449 (1968)
U.S. v. Pate 418 F.2d. 1028 (1970)
U.S. v. Pollard 509 F.2d. 601 (1975)
U.S. v. Rogers et al. 652 F.2d. 972 (1981)
U.S. v. Rundle 389 F.2d. 47 (1968)
U.S. v. Sims 430 F.2d. 1089 (1970)
U.S. v. Smith 46 F.3d. 1223 (1995)
U.S. v. Smith 792 F.2d. 441 (1986)
U.S. v. Spinks 470 F.2d. 64 (1972)
U.S. v. Steel 458 F.2d. 1164 (1972)
U.S. v. Troutman 458 F.2d. 217 (1972)
U.S. v. Trudo 449 F.2d. 649 (1971)
U.S. v. Truslow 530 F.2d. 257 (1975)
U.S. v. Valenzuela 521 F.2d. 414 (1975)
U.S. v. Venere 416 F.2d. 144 (1969)
U.S. v. Vissars 596 F.2d. 400 (1979)
U.S. v. Wallack 414 F.2d. 246 (1969)
U.S. v. Washington 952 F.2d. 1402 (1991)
U.S. v. Wilson 500 F.2d. 715 (1974)
U.S. v. Yeager 453 F.2d. 1001 (1971)
VanErmen v. Burke 398 F.2d. 329 (1968)
Weidner v. Thieret 932 F.2d. 626 (1991)
Westbrook v. Zant 704 F.2d. 1487 (1983)
White v. Lewis et al. 874 F.2d. 599 (1989)
White v. U.S. 415 F.2d. 292 (1969)
Woodson v. Brewer 437 F.2d. 1036 (1971)
Yates v. U.S. 418 F.2d. 1228 (1969)
Young v. U.S. 344 F.2d. 1006 (1965)

Supreme Court Cases

Aschcroft v. Tennessee 322 U.S. 143 (1944)
Boulden v. Holman 394 U.S. 478 (1969)
Brown v. Board of Education 347 U.S. 483 (1954)
Brown v. Illinois 422 U.S. 590 (1975)
Brown v. Mississippi 297 U.S. 278 (1936)
Bruton v. U.S. 391 U.S. 123 (1968)
Bureau v. McDowell 156 U.S. 465 (1921)
California v. Green 399 U.S. 149 (1970)
Chambers v. Florida 309 U.S. 241 (1940)
Colorado v. Connelly 479 U.S. 157 (1986)
Crooker v. California 357 U.S. 433 (1958)
Cruz v. New York 481 U.S. 186 (1987)
Culombe v. Connecticut 367 U.S. 568 (1961)
Davis v. North Carolina 384 U.S. 737 (1966)
Delli Paoli v. U.S. 352 U.S. 232 (1957)
Dutton v. Evans 400 U.S. 74 (1970)
Escobedo v. Illinois 378 U.S. 478 (1964)
Fay v. Noia 372 U.S. 391 (1963)
Frazier v. Cupp 394 U.S. 731 (1969)
Gallegos v. Colorado 370 U.S. 49 (1962)
Harrington v. California 395 U.S. 250 (1969)
Harris v. New York 401 U.S. 222 (1971)
Haynes v. Washington 373 U.S. 503 (1963)
Idaho v. Wright 497 U.S. 805 (1990)
Jackson v. Denno 378 U.S. 368 (1964)
Keeney v. Tamayo-Reyes 504 U.S. 1 (1992)
Krulewitch v. U.S. 336 U.S. 440 (1949)
Lee v. Mississippi 332 U.S. 742 (1948)
Lisenba v. California 314 U.S. 219 (1941)
Lynumn v. Illinois 372 U.S. 528 (1963)
Mallory v. U.S. 354 U.S. 449 (1957)
Mapp v. Ohio 367 U.S. 643 (1961)
McNabb v. U.S. 318 U.S. 332 (1943)
McNally v. Hill 293 U.S. 131 (1934)
Milton v. Wainwright 407 U.S. 371 (1972)
Mincey v. Arizona 437 U.S. 385 (1978)
Miranda v. Arizona 384 U.S. 436 (1966)
Nelson v. O'Neil 402 U.S. 622 (1971)
Parker v. Randolph 442 U.S. 62 (1979)
Payne v. Arkansas 356 U.S. 560 (1958)
Peyton v. Rowe 391 U.S. 54 (1968)
Richardson v. Marsh 481 U.S. 200 (1987)
Roberts v. Russell 392 U.S. 293 (1968)
Rogers v. Richmond 365 U.S. 534 (1961)

Silverthorne Lumber Co. v. U.S. 251 U.S. 385 (1920)
Spano v. New York 360 U.S. 315 (1959)
Stein v. New York 346 U.S. 156 (1953)
Tennessee v. Street 471 U.S. 409 (1985)
Townsend v. Sain 372 U.S. 293 (1963)
Turner v. Pennsylvania 338 U.S. 62 (1949)
Wong Sun v. U.S. 371 U.S. 471 (1963)

Other Miscellaneous

People v. Defore 150 N.E. 585 (1927)
State v. Nusbaum 198 N.W.2d. 650 (1972)

References

Achen, Christopher H. 1982. *Interpreting and Using Regression.* Newbury Park: Sage Publications.

Aldrich, John H. and Forrest D. Nelson. 1984. *Linear Probability, Logit, and Probit Models.* Newbury Park: Sage.

Amar, Akhil Reed. 1994. "On Lawson On Precedent." Harvard Journal of Law and Public Policy 17:29-44.

Arrow, Kenneth J. 1985. "The Economics of Agency." In John W. Pratt and Richard J. Zeckhauser, eds. 1985. *Principals and Agents: The Structure of Business.* Boston: Harvard Business School Press.

Arrow, Kenneth J. 1986. "Agency and the Market." In Kenneth J. Arrow and Michael D. Intriligator. Eds. *Handbook of Mathematical Economics.* New York: North-Holland.

Arrow, Kenneth J. and Michael D. Intriligator. Eds. 1986. *Handbook of Mathematical Economics.* New York: North-Holland.

Baum, Lawrence. 1978. "Lower-Court Response to Supreme Court Decisions: Reconsidering a Negative Picture." *The Justice System Journal* 3:208-219.

Baum, Lawrence. 1998. *The Supreme Court.* 6th Ed. Washington, DC: CQ Press.

Beatty, Jerry K. 1972. "State Court Evasion of United States Supreme Court Mandates During the Last Decade of the Warren Court." *Valparaiso Law Review* 6:260-85.

Belcaster, John F. 1992. "The D.C. Circuit's Use of the *Chevron* Test: Constructing a Positive Theory of Judicial Obedience and Disobedience." *Administrative Law Review* 44:745-765.

Benesh, Sara C. 1997. "Confession Cases in American Courts: Perspectives on the Hierarchy of Justice." Presented at the Annual Meeting of the American Political Science Association, Washington, DC.

Benesh, Sara C. 2001. "The Key to a Successful Prospectus: Consult an Advisor, Early and Often." *PS: Political Science and Politics* 34(4):853-854.

Benesh, Sara C. 2002. "Modeling the Supreme Court-Circuit Court Relationship Formally." Unpublished manuscript. Presented at the 1999 Midwest Political Science Association Meeting, Chicago, IL.

Benesh, Sara C., Robert Lowry, Reginald S. Sheehan and Harold J. Spaeth. 1999. "Strategic Equity: Opinion Assignment on the United States Supreme Court." The Program for Law and Judicial Politics Working Paper 98-03. East Lansing: Michigan State University.

Benesh, Sara C. and Malia Reddick. 2002. "Overruled: An Event History Analysis of Lower Court Reaction to Supreme Court Alteration of Precedent." *Journal of Politics*, forthcoming.

Bloch, Susan Low. 1992. "Marshall, Thurgood." In *The Oxford Companion to the Supreme Court of the United States*. Kermit L. Hall, Editor. New York: Oxford University Press.

Brace, Paul, Laura Langer, and Melinda Gann Hall. 2000. "Measuring the Preferences of State Supreme Court Judges." *Journal of Politics* 62(2):387-413.

Brehm, John and Scott Gates. 1997. *Working, Shirking, and Sabotage: Bureaucratic Response to a Democratic Public.* Ann Arbor: University of Michigan Press.

Brenner, Saul and Harold J. Spaeth. 1995. *Stare Indecisis: The Alteration of Precedent on the Supreme Court, 1946-1992.* Cambridge: Cambridge University Press.

Caminker, Evan H.. 1994. "Why Must Inferior Courts Obey Superior Court Precedent?" *Stanford Law Review* 46:817-873.

Canon, Bradley C. 1973. “Reactions of State Supreme Courts to a U.S. Supreme Court Civil Liberties Decision.” *Law and Society Review* 8:109-34.

Canon, Bradley C. and Charles A. Johnson. 1999. *Judicial Policies: Implementation and Impact.* 2nd ed. Washington DC: CQ Press.

Carp, Robert A. and C. K. Rowland. 1983. *Policymaking and Politics in Federal District Courts.* Knoxville: University of Tennessee Press.

Carp, Robert A. and Ronald Stidham. 1996. *The Federal Courts.* Washington DC: CQ Press.

Criminal Justice Institute. 1976. *Law of Admissions and Confessions.* Criminal Justice Series.

Davis, Sue and Donald R. Songer. 1988. “The Changing Role of the United States Courts of Appeals: The Flow of Litigation Revisited.” *The Justice System Journal* 13:323-340.

Ditslear, Corey A. and Kevin M. Scott. 1999. “The Behavior of Elevated Judges: A Cross-Jurisdictional Analysis.” Prepared for Presentation at the 1999 Annual Meeting of the Midwestern Political Science Association, Chicago, IL, April 15-17.

Eggertsson, Thrainn. 1990. *Economic behavior and institutions.* Cambridge: Cambridge University Press.

Eliason, Scott R. 1993. *Maximum Likelihood Estimation: Logic and Practice.* Newbury Park: Sage.

Epstein, Lee, Jeffrey A. Segal, Harold J. Spaeth, and Thomas G. Walker. 1996. *The Supreme Court Compendium: Data, Decisions and Developments.* 2nd Ed. Washington, D.C.: CQ Press.

Everson, David H. 1972. Ed. *The Supreme Court as Policy-Maker: Three Studies on the Impact of Judicial Decisions.* 2nd Edition. Carbondale, IL: Public Affairs Research Bureau.

Fisher, Franklin M. 1958. "The Mathematical Analysis of Supreme Court Decisions: The Use and Abuse of Quantitative Methods." *American Political Science Review.* 52:321-338.

George, Tracey E. and Lee Epstein. 1992. "On the Nature of Supreme Court Decision Making." *American Political Science Review* 86:323-337.

Gibson, James L. 1998. "Selecting Units for Analysis." Paper presented at the Third Annual Conference on the Scientific Study of Judicial Politics. East Lansing: Michigan State University, October 3-5.

Giles, Michael W., Virginia A. Hettinger, and Todd C. Peppers. 1998. "Alternative Measures of Preferences for Judges of the Courts of Appeals." Presented a the Annual Meeting of the Midwest Political Science Association, Chicago, IL.

Glick, Henry R. 1994. "The Impact of Permissive Judicial Policies: The U.S. Supreme Court and the Right to Die." *Political Research Quarterly* 47:207-222.

Goldman, Sheldon. 1966. "Voting Behavior on the United States Courts of Appeals, 1961-1964." *American Political Science Review* 60:374-383.

Goldman, Sheldon. 1975. "Voting Behavior n the United States Courts of Appeals Revisited." *American Political Science Review* 69:491-506.

Granato, Jim. 1991. "An Agenda for Econometric Model Building." *Political Analysis* 3:123-154.

Grano, Joseph D. 1996. *Confessions, Truth, and the Law.* Ann Arbor: The University of Michigan Press.

Greene, William C. 1997. *Econometric Analysis.* 3rd Ed. New York: Prentice Hall.

Gruhl, John. 1980. "The Supreme Court's Impact on the Law of Libel: Compliance By Lower Federal Courts." *Western Political Quarterly* 33:502-519.

Hagle, Timothy M. 1991. "But Do They Have to See It to Know It? The Supreme Court's Obscenity and Pornography Decisions." *Western Political Quarterly.* 44:1039-1054.

Hagle, Timothy M. and Glenn E. Mitchell II. 1992. "Goodness-of-Fit Measures for Probit and Logit." *American Journal of Political Science* 36:762-784.

Hagle, Timothy M. and Harold J. Spaeth. 1992. "The Emergence of a New Ideology: The Business Decisions of the Burger Court." *The Journal of Politics.* 54:120-134.

Hall, Melinda Gann and Paul Brace. 1992. "Toward an Integrated Model of Judicial Voting Behavior." *American Politics Quarterly* 20:147-68.

Hamilton, Lawrence C. 1992. *Regression With Graphics: A Second Course in Applied Statistics.* Belmont, CA: Duxbury Press.

Howard, J. Woodford. 1981. *Courts of Appeals in the Federal Judicial System.* Princeton: Princeton University Press.

Humphries, Martha Anne, Tammy A. Sarver, and Donald R. Songer. 1998. "Going All the Way: How to Seduce the Supreme Court (into granting cert)." Presented at the 1998 Meeting of the American Political Science Association.

Ignagni, Joseph 1990. *Explaining and Predicting Supreme Court Decision-making: The Establishment Clause Cases, 1970-1986.* Unpublished Ph.D. Dissertation. East Lansing: Michigan State University.

Inbau, Fred E. and John E. Reid. 1962. *Criminal Interrogation and Confessions.* Baltimore: The Williams and Wilkins Company.

Israel, Jerold H. and Wayne R. LaFave. 1971. *Criminal Procedure In a Nutshell.* St. Paul: West Publishing.

Johnson, Charles A. 1987. "Law, Politics, and Judicial Decision Making: Lower Federal Court Uses of Supreme Court Decisions." *Law and Society Review* 21:325-340.

Johnson, Charles A. and Bradley C. Canon 1984. *Judicial Policies: Implementation and Impact.* Washington DC: CQ Press.

Kiewiet, D. Roderick and Matthew D. McCubbins. 1991. *The Logic of Delegation: Congressional parties and the appropriation process.* Chicago: University of Chicago Press.

King, Gary. 1986. "How Not to Lie With Statistics: Avoiding Common Mistakes in Quantitative Political Science." *American Journal of Political Science* 30:666-687.

King, Gary. 1989. *Unifying Political Methodology: The Likelihood Theory of Statistical Inference.* Cambridge University Press.

King, Gary, Robert O. Keohane, and Sidney Verba. 1994. *Designing Social Inquiry : Scientific Inference in Qualitative Research.* Princeton, N.J. : Princeton University Press.

Kort, Fred. 1957. "Predicting Supreme Court Decisions Mathematically: A Quantitative Analysis of the 'Right to Counsel' Cases." *American Political Science Review.* 51:1-12.

Kort, Fred. 1958. "Reply to Fisher's *Mathematical Analysis of Supreme Court Decisions.*" *American Political Science Review.* 52:339-348.

Kort, Fred. 1963. "Content Analysis of Judicial Opinions and Rules of Law." In G. Schubert (Ed.) *Judicial Decision Making.* Glencoe, IL: Free Press.

Kort, Fred. 1964. "Simultaneous Equations and Boolean Algebra in the Analysis of Judicial Decisions." *Law and Contemporary Problems.*

Kort, Fred. 1966. "Quantitative Analysis of Fact-Patterns in Cases and Their Impact on Judicial Decisions." *Harvard Law Review.* Vol. 79:1551, 1966.

Lindquist, Stefanie. 2001. "Cross-Circuit Variations in Norms and Practices." *Law and Courts* 11(3):10-11.

Manwaring, David R. 1972. "The Impact of Mapp v. Ohio." In David H. Everson, ed. *The Supreme Court as Policy-Maker: Three Studies on the Impact of Judicial Decisions.* 2nd Edition. Carbondale, IL: Public Affairs Research Bureau.

Miller, Gary J. 1992. *Managerial Dilemmas: the political economy of hierarchy.* New York: Cambridge University Press.

Miller, Gary J. and Terry M. Moe. 1986. "The Positive Theory of Hierarchies." In Herbert F. Weisberg, ed. *Political Science: The Science of Politics.* 1986. New York: Agathon Press.

Moe, Terry M. 1990. "Political Institutions: The Neglected Side of the Story." *Journal of Law, Economics, and Organization.* Vol. 6, Special Issue 1990:213-253.

Morris, Jeffrey B. "Burger, Warren Earl." In *The Oxford Companion to the Supreme Court of the United States*. Kermit L. Hall, Editor. New York: Oxford University Press.

Murphy, Walter F. 1959. "Lower Court Checks on Supreme Court Power." *American Political Science Review* 53:1017-1031.

Pacelle, Richard L. and Lawrence Baum. 1992. "Supreme Court Authority in the Judiciary: A Study of Remands." *American Politics Quarterly* 20:169-191.

Perry, Jr., H.W. 1991. *Deciding to Decide: Agenda Setting in the United States Supreme Court."* Cambridge: Harvard University Press.

Pinello, Daniel R. 1999. "Linking Political Party to Judicial Ideology in American Courts: A Meta-Analysis." Justice System Journal 20(3):219-254.

Pratt, John W. and Richard J. Zeckhauser. 1985. *Principals and Agents: The Structure of Business.* Boston: Harvard Business School Press.

Pratt, John W. and Richard J. Zeckhauser. 1985. "Principals and Agents: An Overview." In John W. Pratt and Richard J. Zeckhauser, eds. 1985. *Principals and Agents: The Structure of Business.* Boston: Harvard Business School Press.

Reddick, Malia. 1997. *The Applicability of the Legal and Attitudinal Models to the Treatment of Precedent in the Courts of Appeals.* Unpublished Ph.D. dissertation. East Lansing: Michigan State University.

Reddick, Malia and Sara C. Benesh. 2000. "Norm Violation by the Lower Courts in the Treatment of Supreme Court Precedent: A Research Framework." *Justice System Journal* 21(2):117-142.

Redmond, Karen. 1996. "Record-Setting Workloads Confront Federal Judges." [Online] Available http:\\www.uscourts.gov\Press_Release\workld.htm, June 24, 1996.

Reid, Traciel V. 1987. "Judicial Policy-Making and Implementation: An Empirical Examination." *Western Political Quarterly* 41:509-527.

Richardson, Richard J. and Kenneth N. Vines 1970. *The Politics of Federal Courts: Lower Courts in the United States*. Boston: Little, Brown and Company.

Ringel, William E. 1966. *Arrests, Searches, Confessions.* Jamaica, NY: Gould Publications.

Romans, Neil T. 1974. "The Role of State Supreme Courts in Judicial Policy Making: Escobedo, Miranda and the Use of Judicial Impact Analysis." *Western Political Quarterly* 27:38-59.

Rutledge, Devallis. 1994. *Criminal Interrogation: Law and Tactics.* Placerville, CA: Copperhouse Publishing Company.

Sanders, Francine. 1995. "Brown v. Board of Education: An Empirical Reexamination of Its Effects on Federal District Courts." *Law and Society Review* 29:731-756.

Schafer, William J., III. 1968. *Confessions and Statements.* Springfield, IL: Charles C. Thomas, Publisher.

Segal, Jeffrey A. 1984. "Predicting Supreme Court Cases Probabilistically: The Search and Seizure Cases, 1962-1981." *American Political Science Review.* 78:891-900.

Segal, Jeffrey A. 1986. "Supreme Court Justices as Human Decision Makers: An Individual-Level Analysis of the Search and Seizure Cases." *Journal of Politics.* 48:938-955.

Segal, Jeffrey A. and Albert D. Cover. 1989. "Ideological Values and the Votes of U.S. Supreme Court Justices." *American Political Science Review* 83:557-564.

Segal, Jeffrey A., Lee Epstein, Charles M. Cameron and Harold J. Spaeth. 1995. "Ideological values and the votes of U.S. Supreme Court Justices Revisited." *The Journal of Politics* 57:812-823.

Segal, Jeffrey A. and Harold H. Spaeth. 1993. *The Supreme Court and the Attitudinal Model.* New York: Cambridge University Press.

Segal, Jeffrey A., Donald R. Songer, Charles M. Cameron. 1995. "Decision Making on the U.S. Courts of Appeals." In Lee Epstein, ed. *Contemplating Courts.* 1995. Washington, D.C.: CQ Press, Inc.

Sheehan, Reginald S., William Mishler and Donald R. Songer. 1992. "Ideology, Status, and the Differential Success of Direct Parties Before the Supreme Court." *American Political Science Review* 86:464-471.

Shepsle, Kenneth A. and Mark S. Bonchek. 1997. *Analyzing Politics: Rationality, Behavior, and Institutions.* New York: W.W. Norton.

Songer, Donald R. 1987a. "Case Selection in Judicial Impact Research." *The Western Political Quarterly.* 41:569-584.

Songer, Donald R. 1987b. "The Impact of the Supreme Court on Trends in Economic Policy Making in the United States Courts of Appeals." *The Journal of Politics* 49:830-841.

Songer, Donald R. and Susan Davis. 1989. "The Impact of Party and Region on Voting Decisions in the United States Courts of Appeals, 1955-1986." *The Western Political Quarterly* 43:317-333.

Songer, Donald R. and Susan Haire. 1992. "Integrating Alternative Approaches to the Study of Judicial Voting: Obscenity Cases in the United States Court of Appeals." *American Journal of Political Science.* 36:963-982.

Songer, Donald R. and Reginald S. Sheehan. 1990. "Supreme Court Impact on Compliance and Outcomes: *Miranda* and *New York Times* in the United States Courts of Appeals." *Western Political Quarterly.* 43:297-319.

Songer, Donald R., Jeffrey A. Segal, and Charles M. Cameron. 1994. "The Hierarchy of Justice: Testing a Principal-Agent Model of Supreme Court-Circuit Court Interactions." *American Journal of Political Science.* 38:673-696.

Spaeth, Harold J. 2002. *The Supreme Court Judicial Database and the Expanded Supreme Court Database.* Program for Law and Judicial Politics, Michigan State University. http://www.ssc.msu.edu/~pls/pljp.

Spriggs, James and Thomas Hansford. 1999. "Measuring Legal Change: The Reliability and Validity of Shepard's Citation." *Political Research Quarterly* 53(2):327-341.

Stephens, Otis H., Jr. 1973. *The Supreme Court and Confessions of Guilt.* Knoxville: The University of Tennessee Press.

Stevens, Joe B. 1993. *The Economics of Collective Choice.* Boulder: Westview Press.

Stidham, Ronald and Robert A. Carp 1982. "Trial Courts' Responses to Supreme Court Policy Changes." *Law and Policy Quarterly* 4:215-234.

Tarr, G. Alan. 1977. *Judicial Impact and State Supreme Courts.* Lexington, MA: Lexington Books.

Ulmer, S. Sidney. 1963. "Quantitative Analysis of Judicial Processes: Some Practical and Theoretical Applications." *Law and Contemporary Problems.* 28:164-176.

Van Meter, C.H. 1973. *Principles of Police Interrogation.* Springfield, IL: Thomas.

Wasby, Stephen L. 1970. *The Impact of the United States Supreme Court: Some Perspectives.* Homewood, IL: Dorsey Press.

Wasby, Stephen L. 1972. "The Pure and the Prurient: The Supreme Court, Obscenity, and Oregon Policy." In David H. Everson, ed. *The Supreme Court as Policy-Maker: Three Studies on the Impact of Judicial Decisions.* 2nd Edition. Carbondale, IL: Public Affairs Research Bureau.

Wasby, Stephen L. 1973. "The Communication of the Supreme Court's Criminal Procedure Decisions: A Preliminary Mapping." *Villanova Law Review* 18:1086.

Wasby, Stephen L. 1992. "Blackmun, Harry Andrew." In *The Oxford Companion to the Supreme Court of the United States.* Kermit L. Hall, Editor. New York: Oxford University Press.

Wasby, Stephen L. 1999. "Internal court procedure." Email to the Law and Courts Discussion List (lawcourts-l@usc.edu). Howard Gillman, Moderator. Sponsored by the Law and Courts Section of the American Political Science Association.

White, Harrison C. 1985. "Agency as Control." In John W. Pratt and Richard J. Zeckhauser, eds. 1985. *Principals and Agents: The Structure of Business.* Boston: Harvard Business School Press.

Wigmore, John Henry. 1942. *Wigmore's Code of the Rules of Evidence in Trials at Law.* Boston: Little, Brown and Company.

Wrightsman, Lawrence S. and Saul M. Kassin. 1993. *Confessions in the Courtroom.* Newbury Park: Sage Publications.

Zuk, Gary, Deborah J. Barrow, Gerard S. Gryski. Auburn University. *A Mulit-User Data Base on the Attributes of U.S. Appeals Court Judges, 1801-1994.* NSF Grant #SBR-93-11999.

Index